# The Story of Freedom Movement

The Swarajya is our birth-right and I will have it.

***—Lokmanya Bal Gangadhar Tilak***

No price is too great for the freedom of our motherland.

***—Jawahar Lal Nehru***

Give me blood and I shall get you freedom.

***—Subhash Chandra Bose***

# The Story of Freedom Movement

Rajendra Mohan Bhatnagar

Vani Book Company

Vani Book Company

Head Office

*4695, 21-A, Daryaganj, New Delhi 110 002, India*
Phone: +91 11 23273167 Fax : +91 11 23275710

Registered Bookstores and Offices

*Ashok Rajpath, Patna 800 004, Bihar*

*Coffee House Campus, Mahatma Gandhi Marg, Allahabad 211 001, Uttar Pradesh*

*Mahatma Gandhi International Hindi University, Wardha 442 001, Maharashtra*

*Goripur Taliya Para, 313, R.B.C. Road 24- Parganas (North) Kolkata 743 166, West Bengal*

www.vaniprakashan.com
marketing@vaniprakashan.in
sales@vaniprakashan.in

The Story of Freedom Movement
*by* Rajendra Mohan Bhatnagar

ISBN : 978-93-5229-857-0
Story



First Edition 2022

Price : ₹ 325



*Printed and bound in India at R. Tek Offset Printers, Delhi-110 032*

*Vani Prakashan's signature motif is created by Artist Maqbool Fida Husain*

**Dear Children and Young Readers,**

I have pleasure in presenting the story of freedom struggle of India.

Our country had been slave of many nations. It has tolerated torture of these foreign nations. Slavery is a blot on human race which divests the right of a being human in his life time and pushes him to the darkness.

The first and foremost pre requisite of being a human is that he should feel the freedom and secondly he should see that freedom of others is not hampered by his direct or indirect action.

You are born in an independent country. You do not have any inkling of slavery, but we cannot imagine the torture that our people have been facing for hundreds of years.

This is the history of Freedom Movement of India. History is a mirror from which we can see our past and present and should read our future. History is not only the story of past, but also the base of present and the imagination of future.

We have achieved independence after many sacrifices and very long struggle. But we are forgetting the value of independence which we have achieved after many hardships. Do we have the character and determination of these greatmen who have sacrificed their lives for the sake of future generations or we lack this courage and sacrifice ?

Today, it is time to tell you the story of the hardships of slavery so that you can value independence.

Freedom is the greatest asset, preserve it with all your might.

I have full faith in the younger generation that they will protect their independence and the sacrifices of our predecessors. Do not let it go in vain.

Yours

**—Rajendra Mohan Bhatnagar**

# Contents

# 1 The Coming of the Europeans

## The English

The coming of the British was a very unfortunate event in the history of India. When we turn the pages of history of this period, we are filled with anger and shame that a handful of white traders, who probably could not earn livelihood in their own country, kept thousands of Indians under subjugation.

Captain Hawkins is considered to be the first britisher to have landed on Indian shore during the reign of Jahangir. Even before Hawkins many britishers had travelled to India, but the coming of Hawkins is regarded as a historical event because he came to India with a specific mission.

Hawkins arrived at the Mughal Court in Agra in April 1609. He had brought with him a letter from Emperor James for Akbar seeking permission to build trade

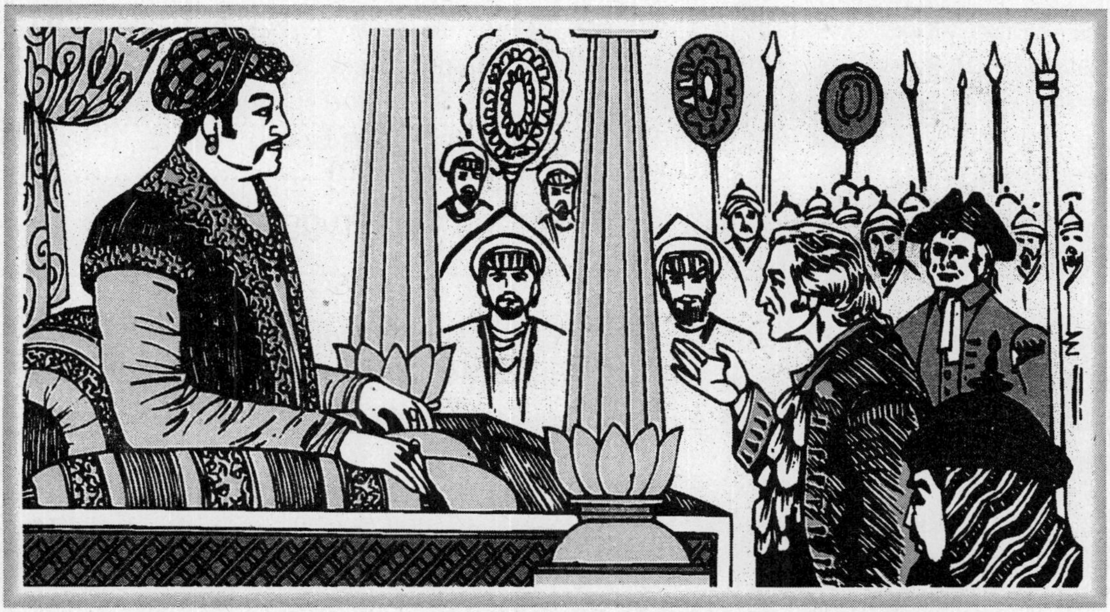

facilities in Surat. The people of England had not heard the news of Akbar's death. Jahangir gave him a warm welcome.

The Portuguese however, who had come to India much earlier won the favour of the courtiers in Surat and Agra and made Jahangir to order the British to leave India. But Hawkins with the help of Sir Henry Middleton obtained permission from Jahangir to build trade facilities (kothies) in Surat, in order to carry on trade, and also convinced him to keep a representative at the Mughal court. The emperor of England appointed Sir Thomas Roe as Britain's first representative in the Mughal court. He soon became a favourite of Jahangir.

In February 1619 he left India for England. But before going he obtained permission from Jahangir to set up factories in India.

On 31 December 1600 A.D., Queen Elizabeth had authorised the East India Company to establish trade relations with the Eastern countries. At that time the Company had a capital of $ 68,373. It was established by 217 partners on 31 December, 1600.

The motive behind the establishment of this Company was to earn profits by employing clever and cunning people. The result was that within a year the Company's profits doubled.

Everybody knows that many other European traders had come to India long before the Britishers came. Ever since the arrival of the Portuguese in 1510, the Europeans have plundered a vast amount of wealth along with committing many crimes. These people fought among themselves and also toppled and trapped the Indian kings to establish their own power in India. There is no doubt that because of the rivalry, lack of foresight and laziness of the Indian kings, India remained in eclipse, not only from 1510 to 1763, when the Portuguese dominated *i.e.*, for 250 years, but also from 1763 to 1947 under the British rule *i.e.*, the next 180 years.

## The Portuguese

In 1487, Vasco-da-Gama reached Mozambique in Africa under the patronage of the Portuguese King Emanuel and landed at Calicut (India) on 22 May, 1488. He stayed in India for three months and was received royally by Jamarin, the King of Calicut.

The Arabs of Calicut and Cochin who had come here to trade with India resented the coming of the Portuguese. But they were no match to the Portuguese who had superior artillery.

When Vasco-da-Gama set foot on Indian soil for the second time, he had a definite plan. Despite strong opposition from the Arabs he established trade centres at Calicut and Cochin. King Jamarin attacked the Portuguese at Cochin but had to face a humiliating defeat.

The first Viceroy of the Portuguese-occupied land, De Almada, was, however, defeated and killed by the Arabs in 1509.

After De Almada, Albuquerque became the Viceroy. He was clever, intelligent and ambitious and is regarded as the founder of the Portuguese Empire in India. After conquering Goa in 1510, he conquered Malacca and Omarg and appointed Portuguese officers in the administration. He was very respectful to the Hindus but disrespected the Muslims. He encouraged the Portuguese to marry Hindu women. Albuquerque was equally popular among the Portuguese as well as the Hindus. He died in 1515.

The Portuguese continued to extend their power and succeeded in bringing Daman and Diu under their control. Control over Goa increased the Portuguese power in India but spoiled their relations with Bijapur.

The coming of the Portuguese however, did not influence the Indian politics much. In India they could not sell anything other than cosmetics and some modern European articles, but, they established large scale trade of pepper to the European market.

The Portuguese power gradually declined, and by 1508 excepting Goa, Daman and Diu, they lost hold over all other Indian territories.

## The Dutch

In 1592, a business sect of Amsterdam founded a trading company and in 1595 Cornilius Houtman left for India. He returned to his country after two years and brought vast treasures with him. In 1602, the Dutch East India Company was established consolidating several Dutch companies trading with India. This Company enjoyed the monopoly of trading with Eastern India. They were allowed to keep armed troops, sign pacts, build fortresses, and bring colonies under their subjection.

In the beginning the British and the Dutch were friendly as both were Protestants. But soon both the Dutch and the British aimed at monopolising the trade in India. This resulted in a fierce battle between the Dutch and the British in 1623 at Amboyna in which the latter was defeated. The Dutch also snatched the province of Malacca from the Portuguese. In 1658, they conquered Sri Lanka, too. However even after annexing the coastal areas of Madras (Tamilnadu), the power of the Dutch did not improve significantly.

The Danes (natives of Denmark), also came to India like the other European traders. They conquered Sriampur, Tanjore and Travancore. But, this did not satisfy them so they sold their Indian colonies to Britain and left India.

The entire Europe had set their eyes on India and her wealth at that time. India at that time was prosperous in trade and commerce. In the beginning the ships made in India were considered to be the best. Even Counte, the famous traveller, wrote that he had never seen such enormous ships which he had seen in India. Most of the ships used by China, Japan and South Africa at that time were Indian made.

India was also the home of silk and cotton cloth which were exported to Turkey, Iran, Arabia, Thailand, Africa, Abyssinia, America and England. The markets of Sri Lanka, Burma, Malaya, China, Japan and Philippines sold Indian cloth. There was no match to Indian textiles anywhere in the world for its texture and

durability. But, the Europeans were only attracted towards India's great wealth and were engaged in fulfilling their selfish motives in some way or the other.

The French emperor Louis empowered the French East India Company to trade with the East. In 1664 another company was established under the leadership of Colbert and Louis XIV. The reason for it was that the First French East India Company had completely failed. The new Company enjoyed full patronage of the French Government. It also took over charge of the security of the French-occupied provinces of India.

In December 1667, the Director General of the Company got its first factory in Surat, and another at Masulipatam after two years. The Nawab of Golkunda not only extended his full co-operation but also gave relaxations in the export duty.

Francis Martin was the second Director General of this company. He was the founder of the city of Pondicherry. Later he also became the Governor of Pondicherry. By 1739, Balasore Mahe (on the coast of Malabar) Chandan Nagar, Kasim Bazaar and Karikal on the Coromandel coast came under the French control.

In this way the Europeans paved the way for trade in India. They took advantage of the internal conflicts among the Indian rulers and served their selfish motives through cunningness.

The English rule in India was marked by tyranny It is said that nothing could be meaner than the policies, totally contrary to the Christian ethics, which the British adopted to take possession of India.

# 2 Conflict Amongst the European Companies

Conflict soon arose between the various European companies because each one wanted to monopolise the trade. British East India Company was a non-government body, quite opposed to the French East India Company which patronized by the French Government. The British East India Company was however stronger and more efficient.

Three battles were fought between the British and the French companies in the South.

## The First Anglo-French War

At the first Anglo-French war (1746-48), Dupleix was the Governor of Pondicherry. He sought help from La Bourdonnais, the Governor of Mauritius and reached the coast of Coromandel. The war between the British and the French Companies lasted for some time. Suddenly the British forces moved towards Sri Lanka. Dupleix thought that his position was firm and so asked La Bourdonnais to lay siege to Madras. The British approached Nawab Anwaruddin of Karnataka. Dupleix promised to conquer Madras and hand it over to Nawab Anwaruddin. The Nawab agreed to his proposal and thus succeeded in bringing Madras under his control. At this juncture differences arose between Dupleix and La Bourdonnais. As a result La Bourdonnais demanded one lac pound from the British and returned Madras in exchange. Dupleix once again conquered back Madras but did not pass it on to the Nawab.

Enraged by this foul trick of Dupleix, Nawab Anwaruddin sent out his forces. A fierce battle followed between the two near Adyar. The Nawab's forces were, however, defeated.

## The Second Anglo-French War

It was hoped that after the treaty of Aixe-la-Chapelle, the British and the French tradesmen would live peacefully in India, but this did not happen. Dupleix was a very ambitious man. He had made up his mind to interfere in Indian politics. After the death of Asaf Ja Nizam-ul-Mulk a dispute arose between his second son Nasirjung and his grandson Muzaffarjung for ascendancy to the throne. Although Nasirjung had already occupied the throne of Hyderabad, his grandson claimed himself to be the lawful heir to the throne. This was a golden opportunity for Dupleux to interfere.

A somewhat similar situation also prevailed in Karnataka. After Dost Ali, Anwaruddin became the Nawab. But the people were displeased with him, and they wanted Chanda Sahib, the son-in-law of Dost Ali, to become the Nawab. Muzaffarjang leagued with Chanda Sahib. Dupleix signed a treaty with both Muzaffarjang and Chanda Sahib. The British had agreed to help Nasirjung.

A fierce battled followed and Nasirjung proved victorious. Muzaffarjung was arrested and imprisoned. But, destiny proved otherwise. The forces of Nasirjung did not co-operate and he was killed. Muzaffarjung paid 50,000 pounds to the Company in cash along with a large estate (Jagir). Chanda Sahib was now accepted as the Nawab of Arcot. Muzaffarjung became the Nawab of Hyderabad.

In this war the French company received generous gifts along with large estates (Jagirs). Both Karnataka and Hyderabad came under their control.

The British were unable to tolerate this. After the death of Anwaruddin, his son Mohammed Ali took refuge in the fort of Trichunapalli, and the British helped him. The French forces seized Trichunapalli, but they could not succeed because of British interference, though the position of the British was very weak at that time. Trichunapalli was about to fall. It was at this juncture that Clive came to India. The French were no match before Clive.

The result was that the sun set for the French power in India. Chanda Sahib was killed in action and Mohammed Ali became the Nawab. Dupleix's diplomacy fell flat on all sides and the French government called him back in 1754.

After this the British and the French arrived at an understanding to remain neutral in political disputes. They returned to their original positions. The British were, however, at a more advantageous position than the French.

## The Third Anglo-French War

In fact the treaty between the British and the French was only an excuse for a temporary truce between them. Both of them were secretly strengthening their positions. In 1756, when the Seven Years War began in Europe and the two once again came face-to-face. The French government sent Count Lele as the Governor and Commander-in-Chief to India to regain their lost prestige. He was accompanied by armed forces. The British had a good command over the sea routes. So, Count Lele had to face many troubles to reach India. Soon after arriving in India he won the fort of St. Davis and brought it under his power. However he committed a great blunder by calling Bussy from the South, because this resulted into a complete routing of the French from the South India.

In January 1767, the French were badly defeated by the British in the Battle of Wandiwash. Bussy was arrested and Count Lele surrendered. After the Paris Treaty the French gained power over the French colonies but the right to build forts was taken from them. They became completely powerless now.

# 3 East India Company and the Diwani of Bengal

The position of the British had become very strong by now. The other European companies did not dare to encounter the British. The other Kings and Nawabs also came under their influence.

Meanwhile Aurangzeb had died and the Mughal Empire had begun to crumble to pieces. The landlords (*Subedars*) were preparing to become independent.

Bengal was then under the control of Muslims, and taking advantage of the British weakness, Aliwardi Khan brought Bengal under his control and became its Nawab.

Aliwardi Khan was a Turk. He was a tough warrior. He had been honoured with the title of 'Mahawatjung' by the court of Delhi. He enjoyed a friendship with the British. The British had requested Jahangir and Shahjahan to exempt them from octroi (*chungi*) on imported goods. The request was not granted but the British refused to pay any octroi. As a result Aliwardi Khan's treasury began to get empty.

The British were taking part in Indian politics secretly. They consolidated Govindpur, Kalighat and Suta Nati, the three villages which they had received from the *Subedar* of Bengal, which form the present site of Kolkata. They also constructed a strong fort (Fort William) around it. They constructed a fort in Madras too (Fort St. George). Imitating the French, they also began to keep their forces in Nawab's areas.

Aliwardi Khan had three daughters, but no son. He declared Siraj-ud-Daula, son of his youngest daughter, heir to the throne. His other two sons-in-law became angry at this declaration and began to plot against him along with other relatives. Aliwardi Khan died in 1756. After his death Siraj-ud-Daula succeeded him as the Nawab. He was twenty-four years of age at that time.

The eldest daughter of Aliwardi Khan was married to the *Subedar* of Purnia. Aliwardi Khan was fond of her son Shaukatjung too, but not as much as he was of Siraj-ud-Daula. Shaukatjung also wanted to be the Nawab. He had the support of his mother and the Diwan (the chief minister) Rajvallabha and they started making plans to topple Siraj-ud-Daula.

The British, meanwhile, had begun building forts in their settlements vigorously, without the permission of the Nawab. Nawab Siraj-ud-Daula disapproved of this and ordered the forts to be pulled down. The British, however, openly disobeyed the order. The Nawab thus found an excuse to attack them.

Jagatseth Amirchand, a well known merchant of Calcutta, was also against Siraj-ud-Daula. Amirchand was a Punjabi, and he was helping the British. With his help, Colonel Canscot succeeded in winning the mighty Hindu Kings and aristocrats in his favour.

At Chandan Nagar the French also actively engaged themselves in building forts.

Aliwardi Khan had been aware of the British activities. But he was old and infirm. However he had warned Siraj-ud-Daula against them. The British by that time had become bold enough to shelter the Nawab's courtiers and his enemies.

This was a critical period for Siraj-ud-Daula. But, he was a man with foresight. He knew he was surrounded by enemies from all sides and took necessary steps. First of all, in order to strengthen internal security he attached the *Jagir* of his maternal sister, Ghasita Begum and had her house-arrested in the palace. After that he took a large army and marched towards his cousin Shaukatjung, the *Subedar* of Purnia. Shaukatjung got scared and accepted him as the Nawab.

Ghasita Begum, Diwan Rajvallabha and his son Krishnavallabha meanwhile fled to Calcutta and sought refuge with the British. Siraj-ud-Daula asked the British *Subedar* to hand him over the traitors but they did not listen to him.

Meanwhile Shaukatjung obtained consent of the Mughal emperor for the Nawabi of Bengal. To teach Shaukatjung a lesson, Siraj-ud-Daula attacked him. Shaukatjung was badly defeated.

Siraj-ud-Daula now turned towards the British and the French. As the British did not pay octroi they were taking enormous advantage of it. They used to give the Indian traders a handwritten note that the bearer was carrying their goods and that was all.

Both the English and the French knew that Siraj-ud-Daula was looking for an excuse to attack them. So, in Bengal, both of them engaged themselves in preparing for war.

While on his way to crush Shaukatjung, Siraj-ud-Daula had ordered the British to stop building forts at once. After defeating Shaukatjung he returned to Murshidabad immediately, because he had heard that the British were not complying with his orders.

On 24 June, 1756 Siraj-ud-Daula sent his forces to Kasimbazaar to besiege British trade facilities (*Kothies*). The resistance put up by the British artillery was not much. They were defeated. The British Officer Watson handed the *Kothi* to Siraj-ud-Daula.

## Black Hole Tragedy

Meanwhile in Calcutta, the British were fortifying against an attack which they professed to apprehend from the French of Chandernagore. Siraj-ud-Daula sent his forces here. On hearing of his hostile intentions, the factors asked for help from their French and Dutch neighbours in Chinsura and Chandernagore respectively. But in vain. On 16 June, 1756 the Nawab attacked the walls, defended only by 250 white soldiers, about as many armed citizens and 1500 native matchlock men. Drake, the President, with others of his council, took refuge on board the ships in the river, and dropped down the stream, leaving the defence to a civilian, Holwell. The place was taken on the 20 June and the remaining Europeans, 146 in number, were driven at bayonet's point into a cell in the Fort, where they had to pass the night, without water, in a space of 20 ft square with 2 small windows. Holwell was sent in captivity to Murshidabad.

Today many historians believe it to be a concocted story meant only to cause excitement and wrath among the British. Their chief motive behind it was to defame the Nawab. Holwell is believed to have propagated this story for his promotion.

# 4 The Coming of Clive

When the news of the Kal Kothari incident reached Madras, Admiral Watson and Clive were dispatched to Bengal to teach the Nawab a lesson. Siraj-ud-Daula, meanwhile, was facing a lot of problems in his state. People were secretly conspiring against him.

After capturing the Fort William in Calcutta Siraj-ud-Daula did nothing for its safety. On the other hand, Clive with the help of spies began to conspire against him. The British succeeded in winning the soldiers, tradesmen and wealthy men to their side. Some feudal lords also joined the British. Siraj-ud-Daula was completely unaware of all this.

Raja Manik Chand, who was incharge of the fort, had also joined the British. The British now politely began requesting Siraj-ud-Daula to again allow them to carry on trade in Bengal.

The forces were all under Clive now. Raja Manik Chand fought a sham war against the British.

The Nawab was now not in a position to drive away the British from there. He was forced to sign a treaty on 9 February, 1757. According to this treaty Siraj-ud-Daula had to pay the British a large sum of money and allow them the old trading rights. The result was that the British once again began fortification, and also increased their forces.

The downfall of Siraj-ud-Daula began from here. He knew that in the event of war against the British his generals and countries would deceive him. He needed some more time to improve this situation. But alas his wish was never fulfilled.

## Seven Years War

Meanwhile the Seven Years War had broken out in Europe. France and Britain were pitted against each other in Europe. In India, the result was that the British attacked *Chander Nagar,* where the French lived. They were the subjects of Siraj-ud-Daula. He was supposed to have defended them. But, he was anticipating an attack on Bengal from Ahmed Shah Abdali, and he was not in a position to face both the British as well as Abdali. So, taking into account this situation, he did not defend *Chander Nagar*. The British brought *Chander Nagar* under their control. The condition of the French became very critical. The French turned against Siraj-ud-Daula. Although, he gave shelter to the runaway French from *Chander Nagar* but it was of no use. He committed a big blunder by not helping the French, and soon he had to suffer the consequences.

The British were very annoyed with Siraj-ud-Daula for sheltering the French and began to make preparations to punish Siraj-ud-Daula. The Nawab asked Bussy for help. Clive then plotted to remove Siraj-ud-Daula from the Nawabi of Bengal.

Clive lured the Nawab's General, Mirjafar, his treasurer, Raidurlabh and the biggest seth and banker, Jagatseth in his favour, through Amirchand. Yarlatif Khan who was a high ranking officer at the Nawab's court had a great influence on his army and was also dreaming of becoming the Nawab of Bengal. The British lured them in their favour. The terms and conditions for the conspiracy were settled by Amirchand.

It was settled that Clive would march towards Plassey. Mirjafar would leave the Nawab and taking forces under his command join Clive at Plassey and Yarlatif Khan would also accompany him. It was settled that Mirjafar would be made the Nawab of Bengal, and on taking charge he would allow the British to build forts in Kasim Bazaar, Khaka and Calcutta. The French colonies would also come under British control. He would also pay one crore rupees to the British as the cost of the war.

However, when all the conditions had been settled, Amirchand, who was the agent of this secret treaty, turned against the British. He threatened them that he would disclose their plan. The British were in a fix. But Clive handled the situation with wisdom. Amirchand wanted a clear indication of the amount of money in the treaty. He wanted 30 lakh rupees. Clive, thinking of taking revenge at some appropriate juncture, prepared the papers according to Amirchand's wishes. He had prepared two copies of the settlement, one on white paper and other on a red one. The settlement on the white paper mentioned the condition of payment as 30 lakh rupees to Amirchand. But, the condition was not mentioned on the settlement which was made on the red paper.

Admiral Watson was however against such cunning tricks. So, when Clive asked him to sign the settlement he refused. This proved another obstacle for Clive. However, he got his signature forged.

The settlement between Mirjafar and the opponents of Siraj-ud-Daula was signed in the afternoon of 4 June, 1757.

Now Clive began to look for an excuse to attack Siraj-ud-Daula. Clive wrote a letter to Siraj-ud-Daula, in which he gave a false account of the hardships on the British, in a most polite language, and held him responsible for it. He also accused the Nawab for breaching the settlement of Alinagar.

Clive neither wanted to give time to Siraj-ud-Daula to prepare for the war, nor wait for his reply. The sending of letter was only a formality. He wanted to thrust a battle on Siraj-ud-Daula. So he began to advance towards Plassey.

## Clive and Battle of Plassey

Both the forces faced each other in the historic battlefield of Plassey. Plassey was the name of a village surrounded by a wall of bricks. The battlefield was 20 miles from Murshidabad.

Siraj-ud-Daula came here with 50,000 soldiers, 18,000 horse-men and 53 canons. Added to this were 45,000 soldiers of Mirjafar. In this way Siraj-ud-Daula had 95,000 soldiers in his army, while the British had only 3000 soldiers. The number of British soldiers was only 800. They had only 8 big and 2 small canons.

On June 23, 1757 a fierce battle of swords unsued between the two forces. The British succeeded in causing disorder in the Nawab's forces. Even then

Siraj-ud-Daula proved stronger. But, just at the last moment Mirjafar switched sides.

As soon as Siraj-ud-Daula sensed it, he sent for Mirjafar. He reminded him of their relationship and persuaded him to remain in his favour. He went to the extent of placing his turban (*pagdi*) at Mirjafar's feet.

Mirjafar held the *Pagdi* to his chest and with utmost humility expressed his regard for the Nawab. He put the *Pagdi* on Nawab's head with great honour and promised to be faithful. But he was only acting. The Nawabi of Bengal had always fascinated him. When could he find a better opportunity to betray Siraj-ud-Daula and become the Nawab of Bengal?

Mirjafar took Siraj-ud-Daula straight to his camp. He then passed the information to Clive, through his trusted man, to attack at once. He had to attack that very night. He told him that he should not let the chance slip from his hand or the result might be disastrous for them.

While Clive was going through the letter and still pondering, Raidurlabh, on the other end, added to Siraj-ud-Daula's restlessness by telling him that the British forces were advancing towards him.

Siraj-ud-Daula was completely bewildered. In the battlefield he saw clearly that troops of Mirjafar and Raidurlabh were standing neutral. Mohan Lal and Mir Mardan Khan did help the Nawab but both of them were killed in the battlefield. Siraj-ud-Daula now lost his nerve despite his large army. If he had acted with courage he could have perhaps defeated the British.

A bullet fired by an Indian soldier hit Siraj-ud-Daula in his leg and it spread panic. He lost courage and fled from the battlefield. Davis, a famous historian writes in his book that a bullet fired by an Indian soldier gave rise to the British empire. The flight of Siraj-ud-Daula caused his forces, to retreat.

The defeat of Siraj-ud-Daula boosted the morale of the British significantly.

Siraj-ud-Daula was later caught and slained by the order of Meeran, the son of Mirjafar. Mirjafar and other men of influence came into the hands of the British.

## Mirjafar : 'Colonel Clive's Ass'

Mirjafar was a coward, and he was also incompetent and unforesighted. He ruled from 1757 to 1760, but his reign proved to be a period of suffering for the masses. Both the British civilians and army began robbing people in broad daylight. A courtier, in Murshidabad, named Mirjafar as 'Col. Clive's ass'.

The gulf between the Hindus and the Muslims was now widening. The British made Mirjafar to commit tyranny against the Hindus. They made him render many Hindus homeless. The British got hold of half of his wealth and finding him bankrupt, decided to recover the amount in half yearly installments for three years. By 30th August Mirjafar was completely bankrupt.

Mirjafar was a narrow-minded religious bigot. The ruler of the Bihar region was a well wisher of Aliwardi Khan. He was not especially against Mirjafar. But, Clive at this time spread a rumour that Ram Narayan was intending to attack Mirjafar. This gave coward Mirjafar a tremendous jolt. Clive offered to help Mirjafar. But he had no wealth, so Clive asked for Bardwan and the right to collect land revenue from Hugli in return.

He encamped in Patna for four months with a large army. He charged the maintenance cost of the soldiers from the Nawab and returned without fighting the battle. He made the Nawab and Ram Narayan sign a treaty. According to this treaty, Mirjafar's son Miran was accepted as Nawab only nominally.

Mirjafar had been badly troubled by the British. So, he requested the Dutch in 1759 to attack the British. The Dutch were also fearful of the growing influence of the British. However, at the battle of Biddera, the Dutch could not withstand the war strategy of the British and were defeated. They were forced to sign treaties under which they could not keep armed forces. They were allowed to keep only 125 soldiers to guard their factories.

By 1760, Clive's influence had spread far and wide. On 25th February 1760, Clive returned to England, and Holwell took over. For Mirjafar the situation worsened. Every British official expected personal gifts from the Nawab. Bribery had become the custom of the day.

Now the Nawab had to face the attack of Ali Gohar. The year, 1760 marked the end of the Mughal Empire, and Ali Gohar gained the throne of Delhi.

## The Rise of Mir Kasim

The British now began to conspire to remove Mirjafar, for they could not expect much from him. His son Meeran had also died. Encouraged by the British, Mirjafar's son-in-law, Mir Kasim began to dream of coming to the throne of Bengal. On, 26th September 1760, a treaty was signed between the British and Mir Kasim. It was settled that the British would get the districts of Chatgaon, Burdwan etc., in exchange of making Mir Kasim the Nawab of Bengal.

Mirjafar was now too old. The throne had become a constant headache for him. A trap of conspiracy was laid all around him. Troubled by this and the changing motives of the British, he relinquished the throne and moved to Calcutta. Mir Kasim settled to pay him a pension of fifteen thousand rupees per month.

Mir Kasim earned the fame of an efficient and competent ruler. But at the time, he came to the throne, the flames of revolt were already blazing all around him.

After being crowned, the first thing that Mir Kasim did was to improve the situation of his empty treasury, and also got rid of the British debt. He confiscated the property of the corrupt rebellious feudal lords, asked for the account from the employees who had misappropriated wealth in the reign of Mirjafar, and also recovered the amounts which were due from them. In a very short time, Mir Kasim succeeded in suppressing the rebellions and also succeeded in checking the plunders of the British.

He knew very well that he would not be able to rule without a strong army, and to depend upon the British was dangerous. Although the Nawab's army was large, it was corrupt, inefficient and inactive, and was unaware of the use of modern weaponry. Moreover their strategy of fighting also was old and outdated. So, he reorganised his forces on European lines, and equipped them with modern weaponry.

## The Shifting of the Capital

Mir Kasim shifted his capital to Monghyr as he found the old capital Murshidabad to be unsafe. He wanted to reorganize his army, keeping away from the sight of the British. He knew well that he had to oust the British. He increased the number of posts and the number of soldiers. The British boats were kept under his strong vigilance, as a result of which British trade got paralysed.

The Nawab ordered the district collectors (*Ziladars*) not to maintain any kind of trade links with the British. Various kinds of restrictions were imposed on the British. This enraged British and now they openly turned against him.

The British annexed Patna, but the Nawab again snatched it from them. Mir Kasim set his forces from Monghyr under the leadership of Mir Taqvi, but Mir Taqvi was killed on route. Mir Kasim himself was defeated in the battle of Uadinala. From there he returned to Patna. He did all he could to defend the fort but he was defeated. He escaped and sought refuge with Shuja-ud-Daula, the Nawab of Oudh.

Mirjafar was once again made the Nawab of Bengal, and with this the British got back all their previous privileges.

## Battle of Buxar

Mir Kasim was at first kindly received by the Nawab of Oudh, who was at that time in the neighbourhood of Allahabad accompanied by the Mughal emperor Shah Alam. On the request of his host, he employed his forces in quelling some disturbances in Bundelkhand. So, the two were pleased wit Mir Kasim and promised to help him. The British tried their best to win over the Nawab of Oudh but in vain. The joint army of the three seized the city of Patna and the British had to flee.

Next, the Nawab of Oudh marched towards Buxar. In December 1764, a fierce battle was fought between the British and the Nawab of Oudh. The Mughal emperor did not help the Nawab generously. As a result, the Nawab had to face a shameful defeat.

The Nawab of Oudh escaped to Rohelkhand to save his life and finally joined Malhar Rao Holker. The Mughal emperor joined the British camp. Mir Kasim also managed to escape and went into hiding for 12 years. All his efforts to regain the throne were in vain. He died in 1777.

After the defeat of Mir Kasim in the Battle of Buxar, Mirjafar was once again made the Nawab of Bengal. He died in 1765 and after his death his son Najam-ud-Daula became the Nawab. The British made a fresh treaty with the new Nawab. This treaty reduced the Nawab's status to nothingness, and the Diwani of Bengal came under the full control of the British. The Nawab did not even have the right to keep boats or to set them out for sail. An extra penalty of five lakh rupees was also thrust upon the Nawab to meet the expenses of the British army.

# 5

# Robert Clive

Clive returned to Bengal as Governor in May, 1765. When he came the condition of Bengal was pathetic. Here, the first significant thing that he did after coming was to sort out the political and administrative problems in Bengal and for some time Bengal heaved a sigh of relief.

The British had now fallen immensely in the eyes of the people. Prior to Clive's coming even the pettiest officer of the Company was not contented without receiving gifts. Clive declared the system as illegal with immediate effect. Prior to this, when Clive had come to India he used to accept gifts. So they had a mistaken notion that he would not mind it. But Clive was determined to put an end to this custom. All non-official Europeans were ordered to wind up their affairs and leave the country.

The smooth running of the Company business depended upon competent officials who would work sincerely. The wages of the employees were very low. Clive raised their wages. But, the directors of the Company did not give their consent to it. He stopped the double wages to soldiers started at the time of war, and instead founded a 'Clive Fund' for soldiers who were killed or crippled in the war.

The employees of the company were now mostly competing among themselves in their individual trades which diverted their attention from Company's business. This caused serious damage to the company's profits and reputation. Clive founded a 'Trade Society' for the higher level officers and gave the society the monopoly in the trade of salt. This earned the governor a profit of 18,500 pounds besides his 4,800 pound of salary. The society, however, had to be closed in 1767 owing to a lot of opposition.

The emperor of Delhi and the Nawab of Oudh signed a treaty with Clive, under which the Nawab of Oudh gave the districts of Kada and Allahabad to the British, and five lakh rupees for their expenses.

Under the treaty made with the Mughal emperor, the districts of Kada and Allahabad were handed over to Shah Alam who received the Diwani of Bihar, Orissa and Bengal. The right to collect revenue and settle cases related to it was given to the Company. It was settled that the Mughal emperor would receive an annual revenue of 26 lakh rupees for this. This arrangement added to the Company's power and influence over Bengal, Bihar and Orissa.

The system of diarchy was brought into force in Bengal, Orissa and Bihar by Clive. The Company had already seized from the Nawab of Bengal the Nizamat, armed forces, and the right to hear criminal cases. Clive was afraid of the possibility of increased responsibility, for this would directly hit the Company's trade.

Clive divided the rule into two parts : The Company took charge of the armed forces, revenue and foreign policy. The task of collecting revenue and settle cases was given to Indian employees.

The Nawabs were to collect revenue from the Nizams, and after taking away the amount spent on their pensions, and amounts to be given to Mughal emperor, the rest was to be deposited into the Company treasury. This system was called 'Diarchy' which continued upto 1772. This added to the sufferings of the masses and their condition worsened. The Company secured the right to receive revenue but ignored their duty completely.

## The Great Bengal Famine of 1770

The masses suffered immensely due to the system of Diarchy. The administration had gone totally corrupt. At this time nature sent a calamity in the form of a terrible famine in Bengal. One third of the population of Bengal is said to have perished of starvation, small pox, plague and cholera. But, no concessions were given to people in revenue. Contrary to this, it was doubled. Farmers had to sell off their lands and they were displaced or driven out of their homes. The government had become totally despotic. The Nawab was helpless; looting, insecurity and killing prevailed everywhere.

## After Clive

After Clive, Vansitlart ruled as the Governor of Bengal from 1767 to 1769 and Cartier from 1770 to 1772. During their rule administration in Bengal further deteriorated .

The British rulers or the Company paid no heed to the problems of the people nor give any concession to them. In fact, they became more tyrannical and unjust. This situation continued upto 1772.

# 6 Warren Hastings

In 1772, Warren Hastings received orders to proceed to Kolkata to take charge of the Presidency. He worked from 1772 to 1780. He found a heavy burden awaiting him. The Britishers belonging to the Company had become virtually robbers. Every employee of the Company thought nothing of grabbing ten to twenty lakh rupees by hook or crook and returning to England. The Company's treasury was also emptying day-by-day.

Warren Hastings was to introduce parity, pay debts, and abolish deficits. He brought the system of Diarchy to an end. The Nawab was given a pension. The state treasury was brought to Kolkata from Murshidabad, and British collectors were appointed in place of Indian collectors.

He reduced the pension of the Nawab of Bengal to strengthen the Company's finances. The amount paid to the Mughal emperor was stopped. The districts of Kada and Allahabad were withdrawn. He set up a government at Kolkata and reduced the losses caused by circulation of various kinds of coins.

To make the trade progressive, he abolished check posts, leaving the important posts of Kolkata, Hugli, Murshidabad, Dhaka and Patna. Leaving salt, betel-nut and tobacco he fixed an octroi of two and a half per cent on other things.

A system of five-year revenue, on auction basis, was introduced. One who paid the highest bid was given the land for five years.

In order to improve the judiciary and make it effective, a criminal and a civil court was set up in every district, and to hear the appeals he set up two courts at Kolkata known as Nazamat Adalat for heavy criminal cases and Sardar Diwani for civil cases.

Improvements were also made in the police system. Robbers were hanged. Severe punishments began to be given in cases of thefts also.

The result was that the Company's roots got deepened in a span of twelve years. But the administration could not be improved, for the chief motive of the Company was to exploit India. At that time anyone could seek British forces by just paying them.

Here are some of the significant events of the time :

## Death Sentence to Nand Kumar

King Nand Kumar was the most influential and powerful Brahmin king of Bengal whose roots in politics were very deep. When he was being made the Nizam at Murshidabad, the British arrested him and sent him to Calcutta. But the coming of Hastings brought about a change in the Company's policy. Suddenly there was a conspiracy to make Nand Kumar the Naik Subedar of Bengal, and Mohammed Raja was arrested.

To prove Mohammed Raja guilty Hastings sought help from Nand Kumar. But, after the removal of Mohammed Raja, Nand Kumar was not made the Naik Subedar of Bengal, as was promised. So he decided to take revenge.

Nand Kumar accused Hastings of accepting three and a half lakh rupees from Munni Begum, the widow of Mirjafar, and helped her to become the trustee and caretaker of the minor Nawab of Bengal. The Council, despite several protests from Hastings, declared him guilty and ordered him to deposit the misappropriated amount of three and a half lakh rupees to the Company.

Hastings took a huge amount of bribe from Mohammed Raja and released him. He was very angry with Nand Kumar and had him arrested in 1770 on charges of putting false signatures on government documents. The case was sent to the higher court in Calcutta. The Chief Justice was Elijah Impe, a friend and fellow student of Hastings.

Nand Kumar could not produce enough evidence to refute the charge of bribing and forgery; so Hastings made the Chief Justice, Elijah Impe, to sentence Nand Kumar to death, even though there was no provision of death sentence in cases of forgery.

Hastings was criticized severely for this evil deed. Henry Beveridge called it the 'murder of Justice'. It is surprising that the judges other than the Chief Justice who had also heard the case did not find him guilty. The jury found him to be innocent. A criminal had the priviledge to appeal to the emperor, but even this priviledge was denied to him.

Was this the justice and morality of the British? Clive had also committed forgery, but he got rewarded for it. He was given the title of Lord; and what did

Nand Kumar get? Death penalty. Honour to one and death to the other for the same heinous crime.

## Maharaja Chet Singh

Chet Singh was the son of Maharaja Balwant Singh of Banaras. Balwant Singh was under the Nawab of Oudh, and was a good ruler. People were happy in his kingdom, and also free from fear and terror. In 1775, the Nawab of Oudh made a treaty with the British following which Banaras was to become a *jagir* of the British.

The British always followed the policy of divide and rule, so they first acknowledged Chet Singh as the King of Banaras. It was settled that he would pay the British twenty-three and half lakh rupees annually as tax and the Company would not charge anything else. This amount was very high considering the size of the *Jagir*, while on the other hand, the Nawab of Bengal would pay only fifty four lakh rupees to the Mughal emperor for the entire province.

In order to counter the power of Haidar Ali in the south, it was necessary to increase the number of soldiers. Money was needed for this purpose. In 1778, Hastings asked Chet Singh for five lakh rupees. Chet Singh gave that money. In 1779, he again demanded five lakh rupees. Chet Singh paid that too. In 1780, he was forced to give two thousand horses. He was not in a position to give two thousand horses, so he sent two lakh rupees privately to Hastings, which he accepted. Hastings pocketed twenty-three thousand rupees from this and deposited the rest of the money in the Company's treasury.

Hastings again demanded for more money. Chet Singh promised to give him one thousand horses — a promise he could not keep because of his economic condition. He sent five hundred horses and five hundred cavalry soldiers instead.

This made Hastings very angry and he fined Chet Singh fifty lakh rupees. To recover the fine he reached Banaras with a small army. As soon as Chet Singh learnt about it, he came to Buxar. But Hastings refused to meet him.

When Chet Singh reached Banaras, Hastings arrested him. Chet Singh bore every insult and disgrace but his army would not bear it. They knew that their king was able and devoted to the welfare of his subjects. The British were humiliating him, which they thought, was highly unjust. So, they revolted against the British.

Hastings had never anticipated this and he fled to Chunar. He brought forces from there. A fierce battle was fought between the two. Chet Singh escaped to Gwalior with a few jewels. A major part of it was looted by his own soldiers, so the British could not get much.

Hastings made Chet Singh's nephew the king, and forced him to pay forty lakh rupees as revenue. This was the first time he had obtained such a large sum of money and also his last.

It was the policy of the British to make the kings do injustice to the people so that they would begin to hate him, and the Company could then play politics and extract money from the rulers. Chet Singh's nephew used strictness in revenue collection and the result was that the people began to run away. The population reduced from five lakhs to two lakhs. When Warren Hastings reached Banaras he learnt that there was no one to cultivate two-thirds of the land. No fields could be seen far and wide.

Taking into account this incident, the directors of the Company declared Hasting's actions as undesirable and undiplomatic. He was called an undisciplined and corrupt administrator, who defamed the Company and aroused hatred against it among the people of India.

## The Begums of Oudh

Asaf-ud-Daula, the Nawab of Oudh conspired with Hastings in the fort of Chunar. He told Hastings about the recent death of his father Shuja-ud-Daula and how he had willed his entire *Jagir* and treasury to his mother, and his widow the Begum.

Hastings could not obtain anything from Banaras so he was full of anger. He thought of extorting money from the Nawab of Oudh. He thought that Shuja-ud-Daula's mother and the Begum were trying to conspire with Chet Singh against the British. So, for this offence, their treasures should be seized. Shuja-ud-Daula had entrusted his mother and wife in the care of the British officers before his death.

Hastings, unmindful of the promise, alleged false charges against them. He called Impe, the Chief Justice of the Supreme Court of Calcutta and made the Begum sign the charge sheet.

The two Begums lived in a palace at Faizabad. The British soldiers seized the Begums and told them to surrender all their treasures. On their refusal to do so, the soldiers gave them the most sordid and inhuman treatment. Finally they were forced to surrender their precious stones and jewellery of gold and silver to Hastings.

Collecting a large sum of wealth Hastings returned to England in 1780.

# 7 Lord Cornwallis

After the return of Warren Hastings to England, Sir John acted as temporary Governor-General for about a year and a half. But even during such a short span, the means he adopted to grab money are dark blots in the history of mankind. He made the Begums of Oudh wretched beggars, and stopped paying revenue to the emperor of Delhi.

After him, Lord Cornwallis was the next Governor-General from 1786 to 1793. He belonged to a prosperous family. He had been the Chief General of the British forces in North America during the American struggle for independence. He was honest and sincere. Receiving bribes was an immorality to him and he had no greed for money. The Prime Minister of England, Pit, was a close friend of his. According to the 1773 Charter Act of the Company, he was the first Governor of the British Government. Pit amended the Indian law and gave Cornwallis the freedom to use the power of the Governor General and the Chief General of the armed forces. He was given the right to refuse or accept the advice of the Council. He accepted his charge with a great deal of hesitation.

Cornwallis enlarged the size of the empire, ensured better administration, strengthened the economy, re-organised the police, brought in law and order, improved public services, reformed justice, and founded a permanent land settlement. These significant tasks strengthened the Company's rule in India.

## The Third Battle of Mysore

Haider Ali had meanwhile died and was succeeded by his son Fateh Ali Tipu.

When Tipu ascended the throne he was only eighteen. He was brave, courageous and matchless in war strategies. The British feared him. He wanted to be the master and monarch of South India. He hated the British and wanted to drive them away with the assistance of the French. So, in 1787, he sent his special messengers to France and Turkey but it was of no use.

Cornwallis was preparing to attack Mysore. He sent his messenger to Dudaji Bhonsle. His mission was to turn Bhonsle against Tipu.

One of the British residents used to live at the court of Pune. Cornwallis wrote a letter to him in which he said : "Such reasons should be caused that would put enmity between the Peshwa King and Tipu." (10th March, 1778)

He wanted that the power of Tipu should be put to an end as soon as possible. So he himself wrote letters to the Nizam and the Marathas pressing them to launch a joint attack on Mysore. It was proposed that the territory and wealth would be equally distributed among them after the victory. The Marathas agreed to be a partner in this conspiracy.

On the other end, Tipu marched against Nargunda. The relations between Tipu and the Chief of Nargunda were not cordial. The Marathas did not appreciate this attack. They could not help the Chief of Nargunda. They persuaded Tipu to go back, but he did not listen. Tipu conquered Nargunda and Tittar and added them to his kingdom.

Nana Fadnavis developed relations with Goa and the Portuguese. This troubled the British and they joined Nana. If Tipu had not attacked the small hill post at Nargunda he would not have to fight the Marathas and the British.

"The Battle of Mysore was a cruel necessity"—From this comment of Cornwallis it is obvious that he considered Tipu as his enemy from the very beginning.

Tipu attacked Travancore and badly crushed it. At the same time the

British forces attacked Mysore. They fought a fierce battle with Tipu's army. The British forces got defeated and fled.

After this defeat Cornwallis himself took a large army from Kolkata and reached Chennai. The armed forces of the Nizam and the Marathas had also reached there to help the British, and the combined forces of the three opened a front against Tipu. Tipu did not expect this from the Marathas and the Nizam and he was forced to retreat, and Bangalore came under British control.

Cornwallis wanted to crush Tipu completely. So he bribed Tipu's feudal lords and bought them in his favour. Tipu's faithful European servants also betrayed him and joined the British.

Now the battle got centred around Srirangapatnam, the capital of Mysore. Tipu showed unusual war-skill, and Cornwallis could not win Srirangapatnam. Just then the rainy season set in. Cornwallis could not get the supply of food and arms, and was forced to return to Madras.

The British gave the people of Bangalore an inhuman and sordid treatment.

Tipu knew that to continue the war in the current state of affairs would be suicidal. So, he found it proper to make a treaty with the British.

Historian Mill writes that Tipu sent a caravan loaded with fruits to the forces of Cornwallis with a desire to compromise. But Cornwallis returned them without even touching them. At that time the greed for wealth and fame had turned the British blind to such gifts.

War again broke out after the rains. Medows attacked Somerpeth. This was considered to be the key outpost of Srirangapatnam. Medows was badly defeated in this action and two thousand of his soldiers were killed.

On the other side, Tipu conquered Coimbatore on 5 February, 1792. Cornwallis again attacked Srirangapatnam. Tipu went on trying for a treaty, defending Srirangapatnam.

This time Tipu sent the proposal of treaty to the Marathas. They did not want to reject the proposal; as a result, a treaty was signed on 23 February, 1792 at Srirangapatnam.

According to this treaty, Tipu had to give half of his kingdom to the British, the Nizam and the Marathas. He had to pay a fine of thirty thousand rupees, and promise to pay three crore rupees as war expenses to them. The British kept Tipu's two sons imprisoned for ransom.

The Kingdom of Mysore was now shattered to pieces. Tipu himself got worn out. It took him eight years to pay the expenses of war. Tipu, in this way, was made completely lame. Cornwalis could have easily seized Tipu's entire kingdom but this would lead to trouble caused by the issue of dividing the Kingdom between the three partners of alignment. So, he left the kingdom of Mysore entirely crippled.

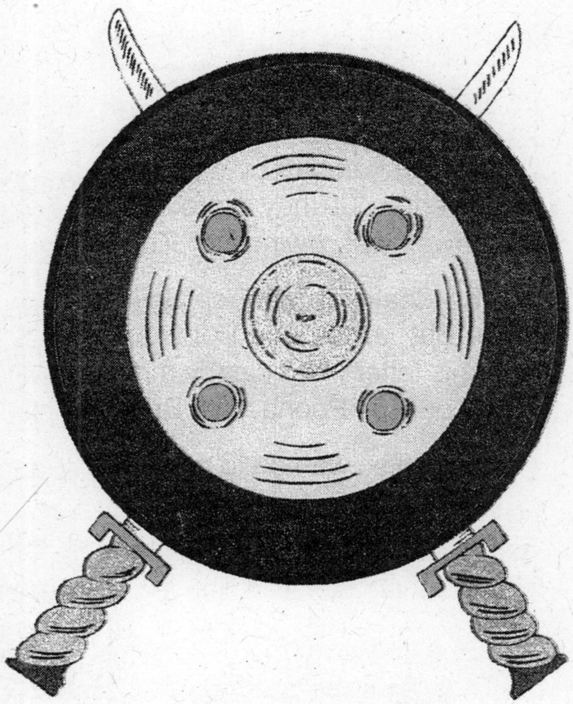

Lord Cornwallis served as Governor-General for seven years. In 1793, he resigned and returned to England. He was able, honest and hardworking. This was the very basis of his administration even in appointments and promotions. He commands a special position in the list of Governor Generals for his reforms and honesty.

# 8

# Sir John Shore

After the departure of Lord Cornwallis, Sir John Shore became the next Governor-General on 28 October, 1793. He had been an employee of the Company during the time of Hastings and had proved useful in several of his secret missions.

Sir John Shore followed a policy of non-alignment and non-interference from beginning till end. The Company greatly benefited in his period.

## The Sunset of the Peshwas

Up to now, during the period of East India Company, the kings, the nawabs and other influential men like them had become old. The Mughal emperor was growing weaker day-by-day. In Maharashtra, Nana Fadnavis and Scindia were still powerful but they were divided. They were fighting among themselves. So their power was dwindling. The British were conspiring to weaken them.

The death of Madhoji Scindia removed the last thorn from the path of the British. But, at the court of Poona, their tricks could not, yet, succeed. Melat, in one of his letters had clearly mentioned that so long as Nana's influence continued in the court of Poona, the British could not succeed in their motives.

The British wanted to make Raghoba, the son of Peshwa Madho Rao Narayan, ,the next Peshwa for they had an influence on him. They designed a plot to get Peshwa Madho Rao killed. On 27th October 1795, Madho Rao Narayan fell a victim to their plot and the British succeeded in putting Raghoba's son on the throne.

Though Nana pressed that Madho Rao Narayan's wife should adopt someone to succeed the throne, but the tricks Mallet played in Poona did not allow her to adopt anyone.

Bajirao did become the Peshwa, but he was reduced to the position of a puppet in the hands of the British. In a way the thread of power passed in the hands of the British.

## The Sunsets for Nizam

The armed forces of the Nizam had taken the side of the British against Tipu Sultan. At that time the British were in need of the Nizam. Now that their purpose had been served, the British began to turn away their eyes from the Nizam, in keeping with their usual policy.

The forces of Peshwa attacked the Nizam. The Nizam wrote to Sir John Shore, the Governor-General, for help but he overlooked it and so the Nizam was defeated.

The Nizam was very angry with the British. He wrote to the British saying that the British troops which were being paid by the Nizam should be immediately removed from their front.

The British were ready for action. They provoked the Nizam's son Alijah against him and made him stand against the Nizam. What else did they need ? The Nizam surrendered before the British and had to sign a disgraceful treaty.

Sir John Shore betrayed the Nawab of Karnataka, and ruined the honour of the Nawab of Oudh to ashes. He also succeeded in driving away the Dutch from India.

# 9 Marquess of Wellesley

Following the directions of Pitt, the Prime Minister of England, the mission of Marquess Wellesley as the Governor-General, put to an end to the remaining existence of the kings and Nawabs. He lived in India from 1798 to 1805 and completed this task.

## The Victims of Subsidiary Alliance

The Subsidiary Alliance came to force during the time of Wellesley. Its motive was to put an end to kingship and Nawabi.

This policy of Wellesley made the kings and the Nawabs completely ineffective as their existence was reduced to nothingness. At first Wellesley compelled the friendly kings to accept this alliance.

The first victim of the policy of Subsidiary alliance was the Nizam. He had appointed many Frenchmen at his court and he was discontented with the British. But he feared them because of their influence. Following this treaty he was forced to dismiss all his French employees and had to maintain six British battalions.

The next victim was the Nawab of Oudh. Half of his kingdom was annexed to the British empire. His army was abolished and the number of British troops was increased.

## Tipu's Refusal to the Subsidiary Alliance

Tipu wanted to take revenge upon the British. In order to take advantage of the persisting war between England and France, he tried to make his relations sweet with France, and sent his diplomats to Arab, Kabul and Mauritius, to gain power. He appointed several French officers at his court.

At that time he was also offered to accept the Subsidiary Alliance, but he rejected it.

Wellesley won the Nizam and the Marathas in his favour by promising them share in the territories to be conquered. The Marathas did not respond to it, but Wellesley launched a sudden attack on Mysore. Tipu lost the battle and was killed in action at the gates of his fort.

Wellesley returned his kingdom to Haider Ali. But the treaty indicated the end of his power as the ruler.

## The Fall of the Marathas

Wellesley made the big powers join him one after the other. He began dreaming of making the entire country his colony. At that time it was only the Maratha power which he had to put to an end. Among the Marathas it was only Gaekwad who had escaped from the clutches of the British. Secondly, the Marathas got busy in enlarging their kingdom under the leadership of Scindia and Holkar.

Wellesley himself admitted about the contemporary Maratha power, that in order to establish peace on firm foundations and to put an end to French intervention, it was absolutely necessary to bring the Marathas under British subjection.

The Maratha Chatrapati Raja Sitara was a political prisoner. The Peshwa had snatched his power. Nana Fadnavis had full control over the Peshwa. Scindia and Holkar were free and undisputed. Bhonsle, the ruler of Barar, was free. There was envy and enmity among the four. During the time of Wellesley, Scindia wanted to suppress the Peshwa. For 38 years Nana did not allow the Maratha heads to split. But, soon after his death, the three, Daulat Rao Scindia, Jaswant Rao Holkar, and Peshwa Baji Rao II turned to be sworn enemies of each other.

Baji Rao, in order to take revenge on Holkar, got his brother, Bitthuji, murdered. To pay him back, Jaswant Rao Holkar launched an attack on Poona, and defeated the joint forces of Scindia and Peshwa.

Baji Rao II took refuge in Bassein. The British gave him a warm welcome. Wellesley took him into the grip of the Subsidiary Alliance. Holkar made Raghoba, the son of Vinayak Rao, the Peshwa.

Baji Rao II again wanted to come to the throne. So, he signed the treaty of Bassein. This led to the extension of the British influence. A year after this Baji Rao II was made to regain the throne of Poona. The Maratha union began to hate this alliance. Jaswant Rao Holkar said that by signing this treaty the Peshwa had sold Maratha power to the British.

Now began the conspiracy to weaken Scindia for he was the most powerful among the Maratha lords. Wellesley wrote letters to Scindia and Bhonsle in which they were threatened. He wrote to Scindia, "You keep yourself in your capital" and to Bhonsle he asked to return to Nagpur. "If you move towards Poona you will be responsible for the attack." Wellesley did not want the three — Peshwa, Bhonsle and Scindia — to meet together.

The British, after a great deal of preparation, defeated the joint forces of Scindia and Holkar at the front called Assaye. Bhonsle was badly defeated. In the end Scindia and Bhonsle had to make a disgraceful treaty with the British, and this marked the end of the Maratha power.

## Efforts of Holkar

The last chief of the Maratha power was Holkar. Wellesley's plan was to defeat Holkar. Holkar attacked the kingdom of Jaipur. He robbed it and asked for *Chauth* (tax) which Wellesley refused to pay. Wellesley had no option but to fight. So he declared a war against Holkar.

In 1804 Wellesley attacked Holkar from three sides. Holkar was a very clever strategist. Before the three British generals could meet, he attacked Manson, and defeated him badly. Holkar ruined Manson's five battalions and six troops. It was with great difficulty that Manson managed to escape to Agra.

Holkar repeated his conditions to the British. He demanded the regions of Haryana and the neighbouring districts of the central part between the Ganges and Yamuna. He also demanded *Chauth* (tax), and sought a promise from the British not to intervene in the affairs of the Marathas. The British government doubled its forces. Wellesley decided to make every possible effort to defeat Jaswant Rao Holkar and his plundering followers.

But the British could cause him no harm. They got badly defeated four times. All their reputation was gone. The Company ran into a debt of 310 lakh rupees. So Wellesley was called back to England.

# 10 Strengthening of the British Empire

## Lord Minto

After Wellesley, once again Cornwallis was recalled to India. But, being ill he could not continue for long and had to return back. After him George Barlow came to India as the Governor-General. But, after the Mutiny of Vellore he was called back from India. Lord Minto became the Governor-General in 1813.

When Minto came to India the Company's position was in doldrums. Soldiers' wages had not been paid for a long time. The Company was neck deep in debt. The people were hostile to the British because of their treatment. Incidents of robbery and theft were rampant in the British occupied areas.

Meanwhile, Jaswant Rao died, but his terror still persisted on their minds. There prevailed a strong disagreement among the Marathas. They could never unite. After the death of Jaswant Rao, the rule came into the hands of Amir Khan, because queen Tulsibai had adopted Malhar Rao who was very young at that time. Amir Khan had always favoured the British.

The King of Berar had not accepted the Subsidiary Alliance. When the joint forces of the Nizam and Amir Khan came to Berar, Minto convinced the King of Berar that the two Muslims were about to attack him. The King of Berar, thus, came under the British influence. Lord Minto sent British forces to defend Berar. Amir Khan had to return from the boundary line of Berar. He had understood the dual policy of the British. He always repented for the treachery committed to Holkar. Minto had the policy of making the kings fight amongst themselves and weaken their power, rather than fighting with them directly.

No other significant event took place during Minto's time.

## Lord Hastings

After Lord Minto, Lord Hastings came to India as the Governor-General. He lived in India from 1813 to 1823. This was the time when the Directors of the Company took notice of the huge trade in the country. Industrial development in Britain was at its peak. Indian trade too was very prosperous and they had captured the markets of Italy, China, Japan, Sri Lanka, Africa and Iran. There had always been a great demand for Indian cloth in England.

The famous historian Laikey has observed that clothes produced in India were beautiful and sophisticated. Calico muslin and colourful printed cloths came to England in large amounts. Realising the competition, the British now put aside the local kings, and ruining the Indian trade became their chief motto. England was far behind India in trade.

The Indian traders weavers were treated mercilessly. They were forced to work. Those who refused to work had to pay huge fines or face imprisonment. Consequently the Indian weavers began giving up their ancestral occupation. The Indian kings could only watch on helplessly. The Indian merchants were allowed to sell their goods only to the British traders.

The kinds of atrocities and unjust means that the British adopted to impose unfair trade regulations on India has no comparison in world history. To ensure that Indian goods could not be sold abroad and at the same time the English goods were sold in India, they made English goods free from import duty in India but put import duty on Indian goods going to England.

Ultimately, it ruined Indian trade completely. All sources of profit in India came to an end.

## Lord Amherst

After Lord Hastings resigned, Lord Amherst became the Governor-General of India. He lived in India from 1823 to 1828. Three significant incidents took place during his reign :

(1) The Burmese War

(2) The Barrackpore Mutiny, and

(3) The Fall of Bharatpur

### The Burmese War

To expand trade Lord Amherst thrusted war upon Burma which continued for two years. The condition of the British became critical in the war. In the decisive war on 15 December, Mahabundela, the General of the Burmese Army, had to retreat.

He retreated from Rangoon to the banks of Erawadi. In April 1825, the general was shot dead. After that the condition of Burma deteriorated and on 24 February the Treaty of Yandabo was signed under which Burma had to suffer heavy losses. The Burmese had to pay one crore rupees as compensation. Assam and Shahpuri Island came to the British as windfall. A trade treaty was also signed.

### The Barrackpore Mutiny

The native Hindu soldiers developed a feeling that their religion would be spoiled if they were sent to Burma. Taking this into account the soldiers rose in revolt. The British did not pay heed to them and gunned them down mercilessly.

### The Fall of Bharatpur

During the administration of Lord Wellesley the British had to suffer defeat at Bharatpur four times. They were looking for an opportunity to take revenge. The Maharaja of Bharatpur died in 1825. A war broke out between the son of the Maharaja and Durjansal, the Maharaja's brother. The son taking 25,000 soldiers and canons joined the British. The Company declared him the heir to the throne of Bharatpur. By that time Durjansal had succeeded in capturing the throne of Bharatpur and declared himself the Maharaja of Bharatpur.

On 18 January, 1826 the fort of Bharatpur fell to the British. Taking advantage of the split between the father and son they succeeded in winning the fort of Bharatpur.

## Lord William Bentinck

Lord William Bentinck was the Governor-General of India from 1828 to 1836. This marked the beginning of a new chapter in the history of India. He was generous, competent, and a man of firm determination. He considered public welfare to be the chief goal of the British in India. He earned fame for his social services. He ruled with wisdom.

He began appointing Indians in important positions in the administration. The British had so far deliberately not appointed Indians as officers. He used the surplus money saved by reducing the soldier allowance to improve the condition of the Indians. But the directors of the Company did not approve of it.

He began to charge revenue from the land attached to temples or mosques. This added a profit of thirty lakh rupees to the state treasury. He issued licences for trade in opium, which added to the state income.

Bentinck's services in the field of social work are remarkable. He suppressed the thugs (frauds) who used to rob people in the name of religion. He stopped social evils like human sacrifice, slavery, and modified the policy regarding the change of religion. He allowed freedom of press, which aroused a wave of mass awakening. He gave more emphasis on education. Following the recommendation of the commission constituted under Macaulay, he made English the medium of instruction in education so that the administration could be run smoothly and efficiently. The result was that the differences in religion, birth, caste or clan, and colour in jobs became insignificant. Bentinck, thus, succeeded in laying the foundation of the English language in India throwing aside all human differences. He worked earnestly for the welfare of the Indian people.

## Lord Auckland

After 1818, the British were primarily concerned with affairs in the north-west of India. The fear of Russian attack continued to demand the attention of the British. Lord Minto took certain measures to combat the danger. He sent three embassies, one each to Lahore, Kabul and Iran. The mission to Kabul and Iran succeeded in getting a promise that they would resist any movement hostile to the British. The mission to Kabul also succeeded in obtaining a similar promise from Shah Shuja, its ruler but it soon disappeared when Shah Shuja was turned out by his rival Amir Dost Muhammed. In Lahore, Maharaja Ranjit Singh was at first reluctant to accept the British proposal, finally that he should confine his conquests to the north of the Sutlej. The British govt. took various Sikh states under its protection.

Left undisturbed by the British, Ranjit Singh conquered Kashmir, Multan, Peshawar etc. He also wanted to bring Sind under his control. In 1831, he had suggested that Sind be divided between the British and himself. The British refused. Eventually war arose with Afghanistan to check the continuing danger of Russian advance.

Lord Auckland, Governor General, became anxious to form a joint treaty with Ranjit Singh and Shah Shuja.

In 1839, the British marched into Afghanistan and installed Shah Shuja on the throne. But Shuja was weak and revolt broke out and about sixteen thousand British troops were killed. For this mishandling, Auckland was recalled.

## Lord Ellenborough

Lord Auckland was replaced by Lord Ellenborough. The Afghan war lasting for four years brought intense hgumiliation to the British government.

But the war with Afghanistan produced two important results for the British. The British signed a treaty which enabled them to trade with Sind. Later they offered protection to Sind against the army of Ranjit Singh. But subsequently the Amers did not agree to the British and demanded that their army should march through Sind. The Amers were provoked to war but were defeated and Sind was annexed to British territory in a high handed manner.

After the death of Ranjit Singh, Punjab became very weak. The Khalsas asserted themselves. The army too took interest in politics. The Sikh Army however suspected the designs of the British when the British looked across the Sutlej.

Lord Ellenborough declared that no Sikh soldier was allowed to cross south of Sutlej. War with Punjab was a certainty. In 1845, war was declared between the two. The Hindus, Muslims & Sikhs in Punjab united against the British. They were, however, defeated and in 1846 a treaty was signed by which Punjab lost its independence.

## Lord Hardinge

The Directors of the Company called back Lord Ellenborough and sent Lord Hardinge as the Governor-General in 1844. He was in India from 1844 to 1848. He directed that only English knowing persons will be eligible for government jobs. He encouraged free trade. He arranged railways, abolished several kinds of octroi and reduced salt-tax. He reduced the influence of the Sikhs. Lord Hardinge also greatly succeeded in strengthening the British army. The other achievements of Hardinge were : He had participated in the Battle of Waterloo, and he also worked as War Secretary.

## Lord Dalhousie

Lord Dalhousie was in India as the Governor-General from 1848 to 1856. He achieved great success in expanding the boundaries and consolidating the power of the British empire in India. He was impatient to annex the local states.

He introduced the Doctrine of Lapse, by which he abolished the tradition of adoption. In 1848 in Satara, in Sambalpur and Jaitpur in 1849, in Balghat in 1850, in Udaipur in 1852, in Jhansi and Berar in 1853, and in Nagpur in 1854 and as a result he was able to annex these states to the British empire.

Not only this, he abolished the tradition of conferring honours and titles, and stopped pensions.

He strengthened the post, telegraph and railway systems by reforming their functioning. He got canals, roads and bridges constructed. He proclaimed that a person would not be deprived of ancestral property on changing his/her religion.

He gave regional languages their due place along with English. He was in favour of making education universal. Universities, established in 1857, were the result of his decision and efforts. The first three universities were established in Mumbai, Kolkata and Chennai.

## Conclusion

The trading British, thus taking advantage of the weaknesses and immoral-character of some nobles, became the rulers. They had never imagined that they would become the creators of our destiny. Our flourishing trade shattered into pieces. Our rulers could not protect the interests of the subjects. Selfishness made them blind to the extent that they failed to realise that they had been kings or Nawabs because of public acceptance, and the masses were their main concern.

We may satisfy our ego by accusing the British. But, the fact remains that whenever the kings are at fault, the masses are also equally at fault. For, it were the masses who had given acceptance to such kings or Nawabs. Why were masses not aware ? They did not do their duty as subjects. We cannot blame any one alone for this fall. We are all responsible for this, in one way or other.

Despite this, we should analyse our fall, and learn a lesson for future. When we do this, the following facts come before us :

1. The rulers of local states fell victim to the British because of their mutual rift and bitterness.
2. A mighty country like India gradually perished because of mutual differences and selfishness and suffered innumerable atrocities, injustices and hardships.
3. It was due to mutual distrust and selfishness alone that we lost our freedom. This testifies that any country could harm its own interest, in this way, and be responsible for its own slavery.

# 11 First Struggle for Freedom

No matter whether he was a Hindu or a Muslim, all joined in the freedom struggle. It was a revolt against the British, against the East India Company. The British called it a rebellion. Later on when this revolt was analysed and it came to be called the First Struggle for Freedom.

At that time the newspapers like Sirajul, Delhi Urdu Akhbar, Sadiqut Akhbar and Tilesme Lukhnow were brought out. They helped in bringing about an awakening among the masses. Eye-witnessed events came to people through these newspapers.

At that time Lord Dalhousie had left India. The British government had honoured him with the title of Lord. He returned from India in February 1856, and on 29 February Lord Canning came to India in his place as the Governor General.

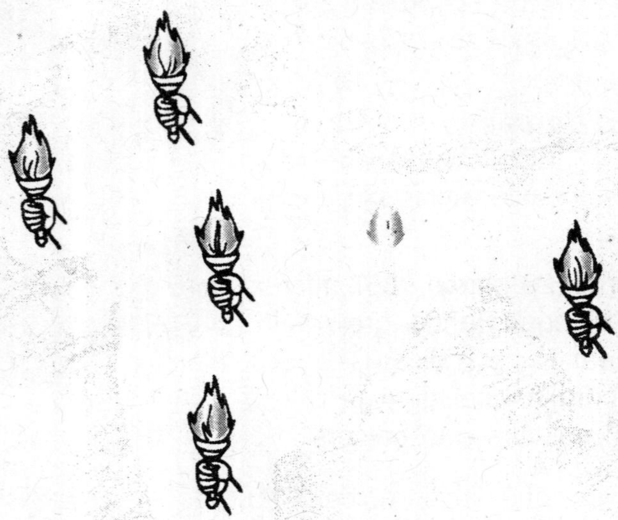

Lord Canning was a gentleman. He was highly educated, polite, humble and peace loving. When he came to India the fire storm was blowing secretly within the country. He knew it well.

## The Sepoy Mutiny

It was the incident of the greased cartridges which sparked off the Sepoy Mutiny. The incident happened in the Meerut cantonment. Most of the soldiers belonged to the Kanyakubja Brahmin community. One of them was a sweeper by caste, who were considered untouchables. One day he was very thirsty. He saw a Brahmin soldier holding a bucket of water near the well and asked him for water. However, the soldier refused him water saying he was an untouchable.

At this the man got very furious and said that cartridges which they pull open with their teeth were made from the skin of cows and pigs.

The news that the straps of cartridges were made from the fat of cows and pigs spread in the cantonment like wild fire. One of the soldiers of the 34th battalion, Mangal Pande, began shouting at the top of his voice, "The British are bent upon spoiling the Hindu religion. The fat of cows and pigs is being used for the straps of the cartridges. Hindu soldiers ! If you want to protect your religion, give up your job. Religion is more important than your job."

Mangal Pande's words sparked a flame of excitement among the soldiers and they swore to kill any Britisher who came before them.

## Chronology of Events

### 29 March, 1857

In the afternoon of 29 March 1857, fifty soldiers of the 53rd British Regiment reached Calcutta. Mangal Pande grew wild with rage. Addressing the Hindu soldiers he said, "Fear is cowardice. Religion is dear to every soldier. The British are degrading us morally, and they want to use force for it. Come forward and fall upon the British soldiers and officers".

Hearing the noise, one british officer Bagh mounted his horse and came to investigate. Mangal Pande fired at him the moment he saw him. It was a stroke of good luck, for Bagh, that the bullet hit his horse and he escaped. He jumped off the horse like lightning, and fired back, but missed. Mangal Pande also jumped off his horse and attacked Bagh. He struck at Bagh's arm and this arm began to swing helplessly in the air. Just then Major General Hueson reached there. He ordered Mangal Pande's arrest, but no one obeyed. He was forced to come forward to help Bagh. But, Mangal Pande wounded both of them badly.

It was a unique duel. Mangal Pande was fighting two British officers, and the other soldiers were watching them. If Shekh Paltu had not checked Mangal Pande, the two British officers would have died there itself.

General Hueson was furious. The Indian officers were trembling with fear. Mangal Pande understood that nobody would help him now. On getting the command from Huesen, they would arrest him and the British would put him to a pathetic death so that nobody would ever dare such conduct in future.

However, he called out to the Indian soldiers to fight them. But nobody came forward. Everyone was terribly frightened. Mangal Pande looked at them and said, "Life is dearer to you than religion. Service is dearer to you than religion. You love slavery. Let it be so. But, religion is dearer to Mangal Pande. I know I am alone. I cannot fight the British alone without your help. So friends, good bye !" He aimed his gun at his chest and pressed the trigger. But he did not die.

Mangal Pande was sentenced to death. But, the news of this incident reached other regiments, also.

**22 April, 1857**

Several bungalows of the British officers were burnt to ashes. This made them furious. Their desire to take revenge grew worse and worse. On the other hand, the feeling that the fat of cows and pigs was used in the straps of the new cartridges was now firmly entrenched in the minds of the Hindus and the Muslim soldiers alike. They believed that the British were bent upon spoiling their religion.

**23-24 April, 1857**

On 23 April, 1857, the soldiers took a vow never to use the new greased cartridges. The Meerut cantonment was the largest Indian cantonment then. It had a large number of Muslims in the cavalry and Hindus in the infantry. Eighty-five soldiers who refused to obey were court martialled and the rest were sent to jail.

**9 May, 1857**

The uniforms of the disobedient soldiers were taken off. Their arms were confiscated and they were handcuffed. The rest of the Indian soldiers watched in silence. They were enraged, but were helpless. In the evening the helpless soldiers were mocked at by all the people and were branded as eunuchs, even by their wives and sisters. Burning with shame they called a meeting to make fresh plans. The revolting soldiers succeeded in winning the 12th Battalian to their side.

There were 1850 British soldiers and 300 Indian soldiers in the Meerut cantonment. The artillery was under the British soldiers. By disgracing the Indian soldiers the British began to think that they had achieved a grand victory, but they were wrong. They could not dream that a revolt was formenting within the soldiers and soon the country would explode.

**10 May, 1857**

The Faqirs and the Sadhus were going from cantonment to cantonment and were inciting soldiers to revolt against the British.

*Rotis* and *puris* made of wheat and barley were being distributed from village to village. This began from Lucknow. They were the size of a man's palm and their weight was not more than 2 tolas (20 grams).

The British officers could not make out anything in the beginning. But, later they realised that at the time of the fall of the Marathas maize twigs and loaves of bread had been distributed. Bread was a symbol of revolt.

The *Delhi Urdu Akhbar* said that through the report of Major General W. Arskin, the District Commissioner of Agra, it was learnt that small *puris* made of flour were being distributed in the districts of Sagar, Damoh, Jabalpur and Narsinghpur like in the district of Gurgaon.

Dhund Pant and Nana Sahib conducted his visits to Kalpi, Delhi and Lucknow during these days. He was moving about to run the revolution in an organised way.

Maulvi Ahmed Allah of Faizabad went to Delhi, Agra, Meerut, Patna and Kolkata also to spread the message of organised revolution. It is said that the distribution of bread was done at his behest.

"Whoever received the bread it was his duty to bake more bread and send it to six other people." At that time copies of the *Kuran Sharif*, published from Lucknow, were also being distributed .

"Under the pretense of distributing the Kuran, the message of the revolution was being sent. Thinking the Kuran to be a holy book, the British would not take any notice and the message of the revolution would reach far and wide. That was the idea behind it."

### Ambala—Important Events

In March, 1858 the government sent 200 mounds of flour to Kanpur. It was sold immediately because it was cheap. But a rumour started circulating that bone powder had been mixed in the flour.

The rumour soon reached from Barrackpur to Ambala. This made the people angry and they stopped buying flour from the market. The idea got firmly rooted in their minds that the British wanted to spoil their religion. They wanted to make them Christians.

Partial treatment was also visible towards the British officers in the army services. While in the beginning, Indians were encouraged in the army services, all gates to promotion were now shut to them. An Indian Subedar was paid even less than a British soldier.

The Kingdom of Oudh was annexed by the British and its 60,000 soldiers were dismissed from their jobs. This developed a deep hatred for the British in their hearts.

Compulsion to go abroad for war was made a necessary service condition.

## 10 May, 1857, Meerut

On 10 May 1857, as the British officers were preparing to go to Church. They were not aware of the fact that the soldiers in the European barracks had declared a strike.

It was not even dawn but the guns begun to boom. The cavalrymen reached the prison house and freed the revolutionaries. There was fire everywhere. Wires had been cut down. Offices, hostels and clubs had been burnt to ashes. The bungalow of the Commissioner was in flames.

At the same time the slogan 'Har-Har-Mahadeo' was rising like the waves of a sea. The joy of victory had excited the Indian soldiers greatly. Their shouts of joy could be heard every where. The revolutionaries left that very night for Delhi to liberate themselves from the British.

## 11 May, 1857, Delhi

It was about eight in the morning when 2000 revolutionaries reached Delhi.

The revolutionaries invited Bahadur Shah Zafar to take the lead. They were shouting slogans. It was a time when there were no British troops in Delhi. The commander of the 54th Battalion, Col. Reple, was hardly aware of the fact that

his troops had conspired with the revolutionaries. So, instead of fighting against the revolutionaries, Battalion No. 54 welcomed them.

"The British bungalows were burned down. Any Britisher who tried to escape was shot down by the revolutionaries. The British were burnt alive in their bungalows.

That very night a meeting between Bahadur Shah Zafar, his Begum and the revolutionaries was held. It was decided that it would not be wise to wait for 31st May. They had to fight a decisive battle now.

The Bank of Delhi was situated in the gardens of the Begum of Amruh. The revolutionaries made it their target. They killed the manager's entire family and robbed the bank. Later they set fire to it.

Now they moved towards Magazine. George Billoby was the guard of Magazine. The revolutionaries wanted to get hold of Magazine. They thought that if that was done they would get lots of supplies. There were about nine to ten thousand guns.

Besides this, there was a large amount of explosives. One Indian and nine British guards were there for its safety. The revolutionaries did not want to fight a battle at that point. They knew that nine British soldiers were helpless. So they sent a message to the Emperor of Billoby, the head of the magazine.

However, to save the stock from falling into the hands of the enemy they set fire to the magazine. The bodies of one Indian and nine British guards were blown to pieces. The terrible explosion shook the very foundations of Delhi. Two thousand revolutionaries died on the spot. Describing this pathetic episode under the heading 'Dastane Gadar', the editor of the *Delhi Urdu Akhbar,* Jaheer Dehalvi writes : "Suddenly there came a violent earthquake. It was so terrible that I thought Hazrat Israfil has blazed Narsingha for the day of Judgement. The magazine exploded. Darkness enveloped the sky, and in it we witnessed the stones from walls, birds and trees flying in the air like leaves."

The revolutionaries could not get much. Only a few guns fell into their hands.

This incident, however, shook the remaining British in Delhi. The magazine episode wiped out all their hopes. The British sought refuge in the Mangauad house at Kashmiri Gate. To save their lives they got into a 30 foot deep ditch and then escaped into the jungle. Villagers on the way helped the escaping Britishers, and somehow they reached Meerut.

Delhi had slipped from their hands. It was now under the control of Emperor Bahadur Shah Zafar. To celebrate the joy of victory, a grand procession was taken out with Bahadur Shah Zafar mounted on a majestic elephant.

However, though the storm got wild in several cities in India, the revolutionaries did not have proper links with one another to unify their efforts.

However, it put fear in the minds of the Britishers.

### Bareilly—Important Events

Bareilly was the capital of Rohilkhand. The 8th unit of cavalry besides the 18th and 68th batallion of infantry were posted there. General Richard was their commander. The news of the Delhi episode had reached there, too. The brave Pathan, Khan Bahadur, had been invited to join the revolt.

At midnight on 31 May, his guns began to spit fire. They began to wipe out the British by night.

Khan Bahadur was declared the Nawab of Bareilly.

# 12 The Freedom Struggle Widens Its Reach

## Dates and Events to Remember

### 22 May, 1857, Itawah

It was a day of the revolutionaries. The Indian soldiers had a burning torch in one hand and a sword in the other.

The British had fled. The ammunition and a treasure of wealth had fallen into the hands of the revolutionaries. The District Collector of Itawah, Hume, escaped in the disguise of a woman. It was the same Hume who, later on, founded the Indian National Congress.

### 28 May, 1857, Nasirabad

Nasirabad, which is at some distance from Ajmer, was at a very strategic point for the British forces. The Indian forces attacked the British forces. A fierce battle followed, and the British were defeated. The Indian forces took command of Nasirabad.

The revolutionary soldiers of Nasirabad and Neemuch moved towards Agra. They were 2711 in number and had 16 canons with them. On the way they picked up the revolutionary soldiers of Kota and Bharatpur.

They burnt many British bungalows, and killed Britishers. From Agra they set out for Delhi.

### 31 May, 1857, Shahjahanpur

The British were gathering in the church when the Indian soldiers suddenly attacked them.

Fighting broke out. Many Britishers were killed. Some of them fled to save their lives, and by the time it was evening, Shahjahanpur had fallen into the hands of the revolutionaries.

**11 May, 1857, Moradabad**

The Indian soldiers ordered the British at the time of parade. "If you love your lives leave Moradabad at once."

In this way Moradabad slipped away from the British control and became free.

**1 June, 1857, Badaun**

The District Collector of Badaun, Edwards, wanted to tackle and suppress the landlords and farmers, because they were hesitating to pay taxes. But, when he heard that the revolutionaries had captured Bareilly and had hoisted their own flag there he was terrified.

At the same time people were told that the British rule had come to an end, and as Emperor Bahadur Shah Zafar had regained his throne and power. Also, the emperor had declared Khan Bahadur as his representative.

Khan Bahadur was accepted as the Nawab of Moradabad, Badaun, Bareilly and Shahjahanpur. Both the Hindus and the Muslims unitedly plunged into the battle.

With this action against the British in Aligarh, Bulandshahar and Manipur, the British now got badly frightened and began to run away at the slightest warning from the revolutionaries.

**30 June, 1857, Farukhabad and Fatehgarh**

The revolutionaries began to shoot down the British in Farukhabad. They robbed the government treasury. The revolutionary leader Tafejjul Hussain was declared the Nawab.

The same was the story at Fatehgarh. The government treasury was robbed. The British who were trying to escape by boats were gunned down.

### 4 June, 1857, Kanpur

Kanpur was the true metropolis of the revolutionaries. The British had made it a cantonment to keep an eye on the Nawab of Oudh.

At the time of the revolution there were 3000 white soldiers and 3000 Indian soldiers. There were cavalry troops besides the infantry. 67 of the cavalry-men and 60 gunmen were British. Their Chief Commanding Officer was 74 years old Wheeler. General Wheeler was a foresighted man. The news of the revolution had spread far and wide. He obtained a troop of cavalry-men from Lucknow. The arrival of this troop gave the Indian soldiers the feeling that the British wanted to take revenge over the episodes of Delhi and Meerut. The fear that the British wanted to convert them to Christians was already entrenched in their hearts. The scandal that the British had filled gun-powder under the parade ground to blow them up anytime, and thus kill them was also spreading like wild fire. This made them even more angry.

The Collector of Kanpur, Hillers Dan, asked Nana Sahib for help to guard the stores of arms, and the treasury. Nana Sahib managed to send two canons and 200 soldiers from Bethur. Although Nana Sahib was annoyed with the British because they had stopped his pension, outwardly he was trying to show friendship. The revolutionaries forced Nana Sahib to take the reins of leadership in his hands. At first Nana Sahib hesitated, but later he accepted the offer.

During the night of 4 June, the revolutionaries burnt down a bungalow. Subedar Tika Singh collected the revolutionaries. They reached Nawabganj and captured the store of arms and the treasury.

Here Nana Sahib, with his two brothers Bala Sahib and Baba Sahib, and his nephew Rao Sahib plunged into the battle. Azimullah also joined them. The Maratha army general did the same. Many landlords also joined Nana Sahib. For 21 days, the revolutionaries kept the fort seized. Guns and canons roared from both sides.

### 23 June, 1857

It was the hundredth anniversary of the Battle of Plassey. It was marked by tremendous violence. Feeling totally helpless, Wheeler waved a white flag signalling the proposal of a treaty.

The fighting stopped. It was agreed upon that the British would surrender the stock of arms and the treasury, and in return the revolutionaries would ensure their safe escape to Allahabad.

### 27 June, 1857

Forty boats, in which the British were to be escorted, safely, to Allahabad were ready on the banks of the Ganges. Sattichaura Ghat was the place where the British were boarding the boats with their families.

No sooner had Tantia Tope signalled to set sail, than the bugle of the revolutionaries blew in the air. The sailors jumped aside leaving their boats. Col. Thomson fired at the escaping Britishers. Canons began to roar and the boats sank into the timeless waters of the Ganges.

### 1 July, 1857, Brahmavart

At the royal palace of Brahmavart, Nana Sahib Peshwa was crowned.

**6 June 1857, Allahabad**

There was a sudden revolt. The soldiers who were on guard on the bank of the Ganges suddenly opened fire.

There was an exchange of fire in the cantonment. The British bungalows were set on fire. The British began to be killed ruthlessly. The treasury of Allahabad fell into the hands of the revolutionaries and within no time the Emperor's green flag began to wave in the air. Maulvi Liyaquat Hussain was declared the Emperor's representative.

But the revolutionaries could not capture the fort even with the help of the Sikhs. Just then Col. Nile reached there. He was very cruel and he began to hang the Indian soldiers. The neighbouring villages were raided, looted, burnt and were reduced to ashes.

**Banaras**

Colonel Nile was in the battlefield. He tried to stop the falling morale of the army. The Sikrow cantonment was near Banaras. The 27th Sikh Battalion was camping there. There were only 250 British soldiers in the army, whereas the number of Indian soldiers was 2500.

Revolt could burst out at any time. The British did not trust the Indian soldiers any more. They made the Indian soldiers surrender their arms during the parade. Then they made the unarmed soldiers stand before the guns and blew them up.

Some soldiers realised what was happening. Thinking that death was certain, they lifted their arms from the ground and opened fire at the British. But their courage soon left them when the British canons began to boom in return. The Indian soldiers began to run in utter confusion. The Sikh cavalry men also could not face the British.

The British searched out the hidden soldiers in the barracks and shot them down.

Col. Nile killed the rebel soldiers very cruelly. He also killed several innocent people and burnt down several villages.

It was the first time that the British were victorious and the revolutionaries had lost to them.

### 7 June, 1857, Jhansi

Laxmibai had adopted Damodar Rao, but the British did not approve of it. But she still regarded him as heir to the throne of Jhansi. British atrocities increased day by day in Jhansi. Cow-slaughters took place in broad daylight. Laxmibai wrote many letters, but the British did not pay heed to it.

Jhansi was also caught in the fire of revolution. Many British bungalows were burnt down. Captain Gandan wanted to take the queen into confidence. He asked for her help.

Rani Laxmibai took advantage of the opportunity. She asked for permission to increase the number of soldiers, which she got within no time. This was what she was waiting for. The revolutionaries began to join her forces.

On 7 June, the battle broke out. The British held up in the fort had to surrender for want of food and lack of ammunition supply.

Rani Laxmibai was made the Queen of Jhansi. She consolidated her position within no time. Besides strengthening the forces, she also set up factories for ammunition.

### 24 June, 1857, Gwalior

Jayaji Rao Scindia the king of Gwalior, was a stooge of the British. The Indian soldiers wanted Jayaji Rao Scindia to agree to be their leader, but he did not accept their offer. Finally the revolutionaries defeated the British. Scindia protected the families of the defeated British and continued to extend help and support to them.

### 1 July, 1857, Mahu

The British cantonment was just 18 km from Indore. The Regiment was under Durand. The incharge of the British artillery was Col. Plot.

In the morning of 1 July, Sahadat Khan, with a dozen of his soldiers, went around telling, "Friends, attack the British. Kill them. Our Maharaja wishes so." The Indian soldiers got excited. So they launched an attack. The Indian soldiers burnt down British posts. They shot down the Chief of artillery, Col. Plot. It went on for three days. The treasury was looted.

The British completely lost to the Indian soldiers.

Meanwhile Ahmedshah, the Talukdar, who was the leader of the revolutionaries in Faizabad was caught. The British decided to hang him. But the people could not see him hanging. The revolutionaries got him freed from the jail. Once again the British were defeated. Wajid Ali Shah was once again made the Nawab.

13

# The Other Side of the Freedom Struggle : The Gradual Slowdown

One great blunder, a historical blunder which was committed was that the revolt took place on a date earlier than the fixed due date. The result was that the revolution did not proceed in an organised way. And secondly, it could affect only one part of the country. It did not affect the whole country at one and the same time.

At different places the bugles of revolution were blown at different times. The result of this was that the British could get enough time to plan their counter attack.

Bahadur Shah Zafar had grown old. He was eighty-three. He was an emperor with a very weak determination. He lacked the ability to lead masses. At that time the British had very firm, brave and farsighted officers — for example Lord Canning, Commander-in-Chief, Sir Henry Lawrence, the Governor of Uttar Pradesh, Sir Jones Lawrence, the Governor of Punjab.

The revolutionary soldiers were not be organised properly. Moreover, they indulged in looting and killing. The masses were very annoyed at this. The British had won over the Sikhs and the Gorkhas to their side. The Rajputs were neutral.

Captain Bernard alerted all the three European regiments — Ferozepur, Jallandhar and Ambala. The Maharaja of Patiala rejected Bahadur Shah Zafar's appeal, and helped the British.

On 4 June 1857, the British along with the Maharaja of Patiala, reached Alipur, just 10 miles away from Delhi. At the same time Brigadier Archland Willson, reached Ghaziabad with the forces from Meerut. In spite of this, they could not face the Indian forces. By the time it was evening the British forces had begun to retreat.

"On June 8, there followed a fierce battle between the revolutionary forces and the British near Badli Sarai. They could not face the British and again the cantonment came under their control. On June 9, the revolutionaries captured the bungalow of Hindurao, but the Guard corps arrived to rescue the British in time, so the revolutionaries had to retreat. On June 15, the revolutionaries attacked the bungalow of Metcalfe. The struggle continued for two days. One section of the British army was defeated.

After this victory the revolutionaries stopped any further action. On June 23, when the British forces arrived from Jallandhar, the British were filled with courage.

On June 30, the revolutionaries launched a massive attack on Bada Hindurao and Subji Mandi. It was a surprise attack which shook the British terribly.

The Kodya attack of the revolutionaries dashed all hopes of the Britishers to the ground. Now it became necessary for the British to abandon Delhi.

On August 6, the gun-powder factory at the Chudiwala Mohalla caught fire, claiming 494 lives. Many were wounded. The revolutionaries were getting significant help from this place. It was a great setback for them.

The 14th day of September was a day of tough struggle. One part of the British forces was approaching from Kashmiri Gate, the other from Ajmeri Gate, and the third from Kabuli Gate. Campbell ordered his troops to march upto Jama Masjid.

By September 17, the British forces had reached Chandni Chowk. On September 20, Brig. Jones captured Lahori Gate. At the same time the British had succeeded in strengthening their positions at Jama Masjid, the Red Fort and Salimgarh. In this struggle the revolutionaries sustained heavy losses. They were massively in need of money and arms.

Bahadur Shah Zafar still had a hold over the revolutionaries. But he checked them from looting the people and promised them that instead he would sell off his elephants, horses and gold and silver jewellery, and provide them with wealth. He knew too well that the revolutionaries not only wanted money, but also power.

But the situation was now out of hand. With great difficulty Begum Zeenat Mahal bribed Hudson and got his promise to safeguard her children. Soon after Bahadur Shah Zafar was arrested and was tried in Diwan-e-Khas like an ordinary criminal.

Now began the downfall of the revolutionaries, the Nawabs, and kings and queens.

On July 10, Nana Sahib, defeated by the British near Kanpur, escaped to Bethur.

As compared to the atrocities and brutalities committed by the British the atrocities committed by the brutal Chengez Khan earlier was nothing.

In Lucknow, the revolutionaries surrounded the Residency. A fierce battle followed. Maulvi Ahmed Shah was leading the revolutionaries skilfully in Lucknow. The British troops were preparing to retreat and escape. They were badly defeated in the battlefield. Just then Brigadier Ho Rochrapant arrived there with his troops. The Gorkhas had also joined the British under the command of Jung Bahadur, the King of Nepal. The result was that the British won hands down and the revolutionaries were badly defeated.

Escaping from Lucknow, Maulvi Ahmed Shah reached Shahjahanpur. Nana Sahib also reached there. The British burnt down several of the Peshwa buildings. Nana Sahib's daughter also died in the fire. The British chased them. Maulvi Ahmed Shah fled to Gagannath Singh, the King of Paon. But he betrayed him. He gunned down Ahmed Shah and won a reward from the British.

On March 26, the British seized the fort of Jhansi, and a fierce battle followed. Unfortunately the Queen's store of gunpowder caught fire and it blew up. The Queen of Jhansi asked Nana Sahib for help. Taking a large force from Kalpi, Tantia Tope reached Jhansi to help her. At the same time King Scindia and the King of Tikamgarh were helping the British.

By the time Tantia Tope's forces reached there they were badly tired. On the way they had to fight against the king of Charkhara. Snatching his artillery and three lakh rupees Tantia Tope moved forward. Tantia Tope did not allow his forces to rest, while they were badly in need of it, and reached Jhansi.

The British attacked him at night. Tantia Tope's men could not manage to flee. Tantia Tope tried to stop them but failed. The result was that he had to retreat. However, Laxmibai filled her soldiers with so much courage that they began to fight with double zeal.

Hume was startled at this and he sent twelve thousand soldiers to attack the fort. By afternoon, they succeeded in entering the fort. A fierce battle followed, on every inch of the fort.

Laxmibai, dressed in a man's attire, was commanding her troops. She had swords in both her hands and was fighting fiercely. The British flag began to flutter on the fort before it was sunset. Utterly helpless, Laxmibai thought it better to leave the fort.

Lt. Broker followed the Queen. At one spot the two armies clashed. Broker was killed in action. Rani Laxmibai reached Kapli, 160 km away. The British chased her again. The British won Kalpi but failed to capture Tantia Tope or Rani Laxmibai. The latter hoisted her flag on Gwalior within a month.

This troubled Lord Canning. After the victory of Jhansi it became inevitable to win Gwalior. Lord Canning's plan was to keep Scindia separated from the revolutionaries. If Scindia joined the revolutionaries it would be too tough a fight. Now it had became inevitable for the British to win the fort of Gwalior, for they knew well that the efficient leadership and farsightedness of Tantia Tope could raise the entire South of India against them.

The British commander made Jiyaji Rao, the King of Gwalior lead their troop. The result was, that inspite of the utmost persuasion from Tantia Tope the revolutionary soldiers of Gwalior did not attack their king.

The British very easily captured Murar.

The next day they attacked the fort of Gwalior. Laxmibai was at the eastern gate of the fort. She fought bravely. Then there was a split in her forces. Peshwa Rao Sahib had escaped. Tantia Tope had also left and Laxmibai was left alone to fight.

Laxmibai held the reins of the horse in her mouth. She went on fighting with swords in both her hands. Finding an opportunity she prepared to come out of the enclosure. She spurred her horse forward and in the blink of an eye the horse rushed out.

On the way there was a stream, which the horse failed to leap across. The British soldiers soon surrounded the Queen. She fought bravely till her last breath.

Tantia Tope continued to fight against the British upto 1859. Even after his defeat he did not fall into the hands of the British. At Jabar Alipurn he was surrounded by Napier and his troops. He followed the guerilla method of warfare and escaped. He wandered in Madhya Pradesh and Rajasthan but no one helped him.

The British excused the revolutionary Maratha leader Mansingh as he joined their side. Being disheartened from all sides Tantia Tope handed over his entire force to Rao Sahib and Fhirozshah and escaped into the forests of Padin. Man Singh however betrayed Tantia Tope and the British soldiers arrested him in the darkness of midnight. On 18 April 1859 he was hanged.

In this way the first struggle for freedom ended in failure.

# 14 After 1857 : The Story of the Struggle for Independence

The mutiny of 1857 ended in failure. More than 30,000 Indian soldiers and 1 lakh civilians lost their lives. The rule of the East India Company came to an end. On 1 November, 1858, the British empress Queen Victoria took over the reins of India in her hands. On that occasion she made it clear in a declaration: 'Indians would be taken into Government on the basis of their education, ability, character and efficiency, irrespective of their caste, colour or creed, and without any sense of discrimination'.

The Empress appealed to the Indians that her own prosperity and strength lay in their prosperity, her security lay in their satisfaction, and their gratitude would make her feel amply rewarded.

## Sir Russell's Dairy

By then, India had grown weak. Mutual bickerings among the kings, Nawabs, lords etc. weakened the country. These people had no faith in the Empress. The Sikh kings and the rulers of Rajputana were, however, loyal to the English. Salarjung of Hyderabad, and Dinkar Rao of Gwalior also shook hands with the English, and even the Gurkhas assisted the English through and through.

It is said that had the kings of Jind, Patiala, Jaipur, Kashmir, Nabha and some other places not helped the English, then the English would have been forced to leave India.

## Bahadur Shah Zafar's Appeal

As a final appeal to the people, the last Mughal emperor Bahadur Shah Zafar implored to them. 'Hindus and Muslims of India. Awake and Arise, brothers ! Among all the gifts bestowed upon us by God, independence is the holiest gift. Satan has deceptively robbed us of it. Let us see how long Satan can rob us of it.'

However, by now, the whole of India, from the Himalayas to Kanya Kumari had been brought under British rule. The public was in fact frustrated with the administration of the kings, rulers, Nawabs, and nobles. The socio-economic condition was pitiable. Superstition and absurd social customs prevailed.

## Social Reforms

The question was now one of awakening the public. To have any expectation from kings and rulers was futile. It was at this juncture that Raja Ram Mohan Roy appeared on the scene. He raised his voice against idol-worship and practices like *Sati*. He advocated widow remarriage and end social customs like *Sati*. He also founded the Brahmo Samaj to reform Indian society. At this time, also Mool Shankar (Maharishi Dayanand) founded the Arya Samaj. He opened the doors of Hinduism to people of different sects.

He opposed child-marriage, marriage in old age and polygamy, but favoured widow remarriage. He always supported the ideas of independence.

In Bengal, Swami Ram Krishna Paramhansa preached the oneness of all religion a task, taken up later, by his favourite disciple, Vivekananda.

In 1887, Empress Victoria held a Royal Court in which Indian rulers, kings, Nawabs, feudal lords etc. were honoured, so that their cooperation could be sought. Meanwhile, the Ilbert Bill was brought out which had a provision that the landlords would issue rent receipts to the farmers, and any farmer, who had ploughed the land for 12 years, would be able to claim its ownership. Exploitation of the Indian people, however, continued. When in January 1877, Queen Victoria was declared Empress of India, the country was passing through a severe famine. At almost the same time food grains worth 80 lakh pounds were exported to England.

But there were quite a few humanists among the English. In 1880, Lord Rippon became the Governor of India. He was liberal and benevolent and brought about several reforms in administration and judiciary. Indian magistrates had no authority to deal with the cases of European criminals. P.C. Ilbert was a member of law in the Rippon Council. He brought out a bill for authorising Indian magistrates to deal with the cases of European criminals. Lord Rippon wanted that the differences on the counts of high and low, white and black etc. must be abolished.

The English rulers were however against it. They vehemently reprobated Lord Rippon. The English constituted a federal body, viz. 'European Defence Federation' and this body denounced the Bill.

Some English people even got hold of a few sentries of the Government Houses in Calcutta and conspired to capture Rippon and send him back to England.

Lord Rippon was finally forced to withdraw the Bill.

This however, exposed the apathy and hatred in the minds of the British towards the Indians. Jamshedji Jija Bhai, Surendra Nath Banerjee, Mangaldas, Nathu Bhai and others were opposed to the British administration.

The Indian magistrates of that time, Bihari Lal Gupta, Surendra Nath Banerjee (Presidency Magistrate), Ramesh Chandra Dutta (District Magistrate), and others understood it well that the British Government was not in favour of giving them impartial justice. This created an atmosphere which was quite conducive to patriotism. Had the Illbert Bill been passed, it would have brought peace. But the very fact that it was not passed was disadvantageous to the British Government.

The educated people now began to raise their voice for their own benefits. The Madras Native Association, Poona's Public Committee and others protested against the British rule. It was demanded that the doors of Civil Services should be kept open for all; the salaries of the employees must be increased and the emoluments of high-officials must be curtailed and appointments must be finalized on the basis of competitive examinations. All this was in consequence of the Illbert Bill.

## Founding of the Indian National Congress

In 1885, Allen Octavion Hume founded the Indian National Congress. The first session of Congress was convened at Pune in December, 1885. Its main objectives were the formation of a democratic constitution, freedom from personal ambition, and it was also agreed that the greatest among them would be considered humble servants to all. Thus, the intellectuals found a platform for themselves. Hume was a humanitarien and was mentally perturbed on account of the abject poverty and miserable plight of the Indians.

## Hume : A Great Lover of Mankind

The educated Indians, press and all the representatives of the Congress Committee made constant efforts to explain to the Government the problems of the people but the Government refused to understand. A.O. Hume reiterated that it was primary duty of the people to bring about an awareness, so that every Indian must become a soldier in the great campaign for rights and justice.

Allen Octavion Hume's father, Joseph Hume was a Scottish patriot, and was deeply interested in the problems of social reform. For about 12 years he had been in the service of the East India Company. Thereafter, he entered Parliament.

Allen began his service career with the East India Company, and very much like his father, he was a patriot as well as a social reformer. He was a great lover of mankind. Hume loved India as much as he loved England. He was in India in 1857. At the age of 26 he became one of the prominent civil officers in Itawa District of Uttar Pradesh.

At the time of Hume, the revenue from the Excise Deptt. of Itawa District was increasing every year. The British Government was very pleased with Allen's work. But the District Officer has to function both as a father as well as a mother. He has to care for the welfare of the people of the District. For that reason Allen Hume wrote to the High Officials. "It is rather painful for me to find the Government revenue increasing. I am sorry that I have been protesting against the present unjust system which has remained as such."

"The present system has given rise to such a section of people who have been horribly selfish and drag our countrymen towards the habit of drinks, turning them into debauches and criminals. This is clearly known only to those who, like me, have bothered to find out the root cause of poverty among people and also realize how the evil of drinking has crossed its dreadful limits during the last 20 years."

As a consequence Hume was demoted and humiliated, while his sub-ordinates and juniors were promoted. Allen Hume was loved and respected by the Indians but the British Government turned a deaf ear to him. This great English man wrote in a letter to the graduates of Calcutta University.

"There is hardly any hope for the progressive life of India, if fifty per cent of your educated masses could not come out with a strong sense of self-sacrifice, with an ardent love for your country and with enough true and unselfish patriotism, so that you could sacrifice your whole life for India in the hour of need."

"The sons of the soil of India would continue to be helpless and miserable and live like puppets in the hands of foreign rulers, so long as you don't launch a firm campaign to achieve much of freedom much of impartial administration and much of rights and privileges in the affairs of the Government, so long as you don't do so, we, who have been your well-wishers, would be proved wrong and our opponents would be proved right."

W.C. Banerjee, Keshav Pillai, Dada Bhai Naroji, N.G. Chandrawarkar, Ramgayya Naidu, Rahim Tulla Sayani, Narendra Nath and other representatives played a significant role in Indian National Congress. Lord Dufferin had been of considerable help in this task. In this way a new and revolutionary platform was found for the struggle for India's independence."

An opposition of truth brings about disaster. In the 1887 Session of the Indian National Congress, held in Madras, famous Barrister Badruddin Tyabjee was its president. Advocate Norton had a chance to address the session of Congress and he proclaimed loudly.

"If it is treachery to revolt against injustice, to demand a just and reasonable Government, to raise voice against tyrannical rule, and torture of the people, to stand up against exploitation and oppression, to pray for hearing, before the punishment is awarded, to demand individual freedom, and to expect and aspire for continuous development, then I feel a great joy in being a traitor myself and my joys will increase to find myself among the traitors."

It was time that every educated patriot had in his mind a deep-rooted sentiment of people's rule. Foreign clothes were being dumped and set on fire. Day after day, people felt a new vigour and new enthusiasm. It was in this scenario in 1905 when Lord Curzon became the Viceroy.

## Raksha Bandhan Celebrated

On 1 September 1905, Lord Curzon proclaimed the partition of Bengal into two parts. It came into effect from 16 October 1905. The division of Bengal meant one body getting split into two. Both the parts were crying in agony and all the people of India had their eyes fixed on Bengal. A protest note with the signatures of 70,000 people opposing the division of Bengal was sent to the Secretary of India. On account of a forceful opposition move Lord Curzon was forced to return to England.

Lord Curzon was suceeded by Lord Minto as the next Viceroy of India. At this point of time the whole country was burning. The whole of Bengal was under storm. It was at this time when the Hindu festival of Raksha Bandhan was transformed into a national movement.

The scene on the bank of the Ganges was spectacular. Thousands of people were standing by its bank tying threads on each other's wrists. Anand Mohan gave the slogan of "Vande Mataram" to the mammoth gathering. A national fund was launched and instantly an amount of Rs. 70,000 was collected.

The whole of Bengal was under Bandh and the fire in the hearth burnt at nobody's home. All the people marched to the Ganges bare-footed.

The great poet Rabindra Nath Tagore composed a song on this occassion, a stanza of which runs as follows :

'Holy is the soil of Bengal,
Holy is its Water,
Holy is its air
Holy is its fruit
All is so very sacred and holy about Bengal.'

## Restriction on *Vande Mataram*

The British Government was deeply upset with the chanting of 'Vande Mataram'. As the procession went on, loud chants of 'Vande Mataram' were heard. The Government had put a ban on 'Vande Mataram'. The procession, headed by A. Rasool and his wife, was moving on. The police were also accompanying the procession, so that the moment anyone chanted Vande Mataram, the police would pounce upon him and beat him up. The procession was fairly large and the people were all filled with unbounded enthusiasm. In this procession people began to sing the song of Rajni Kant.

'Bow your heads to Bharat Mata,

Whatever coarse cloth she offers,

Accept it joyfully;

Your Bharat Mata is in the hour of crisis

To do anything more is beyond her means.'

The people moving in the procession had put the badges of Vande Mataram on their arms. The only condition imposed on the procession was that no body would chant Vande Mataram. There was certainly no restriction in putting the badges of Vande Mataram on their arms.

But the police were just waiting for an excuse to spur into action. They suddenly attacked the quiet and innocent people in the procession and beat them with their sticks. Even the women were wounded by the police. They were put into prison, raped and assaulted. A child was struck with a heavy stick, and the moment he chanted Vande Mataram, he was thrown into a marshy tank. This episode later came to be known as the **Barisal Kand.** It was condemned all over the country.

# 15 The Freedom Struggle gains Momentum

## Moderates and Extremists

The impetuous freedom fighters were treated very badly in the prisons. They were not at all conscious how the day was followed by night, and how there was rain after sun-shine. There was only one fire burning inside them, for which they were running about, day in and day out. It was at this time that Congress was split into two groups. One consisted of Moderates with Ranade as their leader. They believed in keeping the Government vigilant in accordance with the rules and regulations conforming to law. Bal Gangadhar Tilak was the leader of the other group of Extremists, who believed in nothing but direct action. Tilak was the editor of the Marathi Weekly *Kesri*. Both Ranade and Tilak were completely dedicated towards the nation but in their own ways.

## Ganapati Festival

To bring about an awakening among the people Bal Gangadhar Tilak desired that the Ganapati Festival be revived once again. Ganapati Festival was celebrated as a national festival in the past. When the Maratha rule came to an end, people had almost forgotten the Ganapati Festival. Both Hindus and Muslims participated in it. Tilak decided that through that Festival he would bring about an awakening in the country. Once again the festival of Lord Ganapati began to be celebrated in Maharashtra and other places. Plays were staged to rouse patriotism. The British Government had almost succeeded in suppressing the celebration of the

Ganapati Festival. It now began to be celebrated with redoubled enthusiasm. In those dramas it was demonstrated how to stand up against oppression. In the process of celebrating Ganapati Festival there were processions in which the English were called heathens. They were called the enemies of their motherland. Slogans of patriotism were shouted. In the dramas on a large scale, and at different places the scene of killing Gajasur by Lord Ganpati was prominently staged. Gajasur symbolically represented the Englishmen. The students of schools and colleges showed much enthusiasm in the celebrations. At schools, there were exhibitions of gymnastics in the name of Lord Ganesh. Now Ganpati Festivals also began to be celebrated at Jodhpur, Jaipur, Agra, Mathura, Madras, Dwarka, Varanasi, Delhi and such other places with great joy and gusto. The British Government made all possible efforts to curb such processions. At times they even lathi charged. Sometimes suits were filed against the organizers. This brought a new wave of enthusiasm in the country. Besides, in Bengal there were processions of Goddess Durga.

## Shivaji Movement

The Ganesh movement was at its peak. An article about the Ganpati Festival was published in *Native Opinion* with the title, **Demolition of Shivaji's Tomb**. Tilak found a fresh wave of inspiration in it. He established the Shivaji Fund through his newspaper *Kesri*. For two months this campaign went on fast. The very name of Shivaji ushered a new life in the country. The work of publicity about Shivaji Fund reached its consummation in a meeting at Pune. It was a unique

meeting and the largest meeting held at Pune after the establishment of the British Empire. On the peak of Rajgarh Fort, a function was held in the memory of Shivaji. The fort was situated on a steep hill. It was indeed an uphill task to scale it. There was hardly any building on the peak except for the foundation and the walls. It was a solitary place, remote from the township. Such a deserted place found itself illumined that day. Tilak knowingly chose that spot since he wanted to feel the puise of the nation.

Though everybody was not able to climb that hill as it was a steep climb, but still six thousand people from different parts of Maharashtra gathered there. That night they held a large procession with torches in their hands. Huge pictures of Shivaji and his guru Ram Das were taken out. Such a splendid celebration was held after 250 years of the enthronement of Shivaji. The deserted hill resounded with slogans of "Long live Shivaji". The Shivaji movement soon spread all over the country. There was a lot of excitement, specially in Calcutta, about this movement.

## Plague and Famine

In Pune, plague had assumed gigantic proportions. Several places in the country were struck with famine. People were abandoning their homes. Shops and houses were being looted in the absence of their respective land lords. There was hardly any hearing against injustice. To produce witnesses was as good as not producing them. Soldiers were vitiating the sanctity of the temples. Tilak, through his *Kesari* made an ardent appeal to the sufferers :

'When the Queen desires that nobody should die of hunger, when the Governor announced that all have a right to live, and when Indian Ministers are prepared to accept even loans, even then will you die miserably as cowards ? If you have enough money to pay balance of taxes, certainly do pay it. If you are not in a position, will you sell your belongings to escape the wrath of officers ? Will you gather no courage, even when you are confronted with death ? We can face several such famines, but what shall we do with the people endowed with the mentality of dumb driven sheep ?'

There was logic, dignity and justice in the words of Tilak. He was much against the looting of shops. He thought and desired that the collector ought to provide work and food to those who had been rendered homeless. It was obviously his duty. Tilak was sent to prison on account of his extreme views. The English Magistrates believed that the atmosphere of extremism would automatically cool down with the imprisonment of Tilak. The moderates cooled down, but meetings of Shivaji Festivals continued to generate heat and there was incessant fire in the minds of the people.

## Assassination of Ayerst and Raind

Pune at the time was passing through plague, famine, oppression and injustice. On the other hand, in Pune itself, the Diamond Jubilee of the Queen was being

celebrated. The Government House was lit up magnificently. There were displays of fireworks.

It was past midnight. The festival was in its fill swing. Lieutenant Ayerst and his wife were returning home in a Victoria (carriage). Another carriage was passing along the other side of the road. Suddenly there were flashes accompanied by sounds of gunfire. Raind, who was in the other carriage was shot. Ayerst was struck when there was another round of firing.

W.C. Raind was a Police Commissioner. He was notorious for his inhuman and barbaric deeds in plague-struck Pune.

Damodar Chaffekar and Bal Krishna Chaffekar were the assassins in these two cases. Damodar and Bal Krishna were both sentenced to death.

## Boycott of Foreign Goods

People, now, were not at all scared of death. They were willing to give up their lives for the country. There was now boycott of all articles made in England. The whole of India was resounding with the voice of Tilak. The chants of Vande Mataram could be heard everywhere. When the students were given foolscap paper to write out their answers at the Preliminary Matriculation Examination, they tore away the answer sheets. The English Principal considered this action of tearing the answer sheets (made in England) an insult to the Queen. He announced that the students would not be allowed to take their examination until they were punished.

Even the punishment of 50 lashes with a cane to each student didn't appease the principal. He announced that the treacherous students would not be given the certificate of good moral character, and consequently they were debarred from appearing at the ensuing examinations. The character certificate was essential for taking the examination.

## Foreign Clothes Set on Fire

This incident added fuel to fire. Foreign clothes and articles were set on fire by students at different places. A question cropped up in several minds, 'Why should the foreign clothes be set on fire?' they asked Tilak. 'Why shouldn't the foreign clothes be distributed among the poor?

Tilak replied, 'It would be improper on the point of religion and patriotism, since any thing which was humiliating to one citizen would be insulting to all the people of the country as well'.

It marked the beginning of a new phase.

In Pune, it was the festive occasion of Vijayadashami. A procession started from Maharashtra Vidyalaya. The procession went along with a gun-carriage, on which the drum beaters sat and announced at frequent brief intervals :

'Hear! Hear! Descendants of Shivaji! Listen to us. Throw out the articles from your house which are made in England. Collect all the foreign articles and reach the Chatur Singh Ground at once. There the effigy of the Demon Ravana will be burnt.'

Each and every announcement was accompanied by loud drum beats. Leaflets were distributed. Foreign clothes and articles were dumped into the carriage.

An effigy of Ravana, wearing foreign clothes, was erected on Chatur Singh Ground and was surrounded by crowds of thousands of people. Kerosene was sprinkled on the effigy, and within moments the flames were touching the sky. The whole atmosphere resounded with triumphant shouts of

'Long live Shivaji !', 'Long live Lord Ganesh !' 'Vande Mataram !'.

The boycott of foreign articles continued with full fervour and threatened to continue till the orders for the division of Bengal were not withdrawn. Whatever efforts were made by the Government to suppress the movement for using home-made articles proved to be ineffective. On the contrary, it boosted the morale of the people and they at once stopped buying foreign goods. There was a storm raised by people to boycott Government Services also. Minto was completely perplexed. In fact, Lord Curzon had laid a bed of thorns for him before he left India.

## Era of Tilak

It was the era of Tilak. The Moderates in the Congress were weakening. The circulation of *Kesari*, edited by Tilak went up to 20,000. The Government wanted to imprison Tilak a longer time. Finally they prosecuted him on account of his editorials published in *Kesari* on 12 May and 9 June, 1908.

These two editorials had warned the government that if they followed the oppressive methods of the Czars of Russia, the Indians would also be compelled to resort to the methods of the Russian revolutionaries for their self-defence.

The jury, appointed to enquire into the case of Tilak consisted of 9 members, out of whom, 7 were English. Tilak was sentenced to six years. He spent his term of imprisonment in Mandlay in Burma (Myanmar). Here his health sharply declined.

Tilak's imprisonment gave rise to a lot of unrest all over India. The labourers in Bombay went on strike. A bandh was observed in Bombay. The moment an Englishman was observed anywhere, he would be beaten up. Wine shops were smashed. Schools and colleges were closed down. In several places innocent people were lathi-charged and fired upon. The suppressive activities of the Government became all the more intense.

People were now frustrated with the Congress. They were in favour of bombs. They began to consider the Congress as a bogey that did nothing except pass resolutions.

## Revolutionary Activities

The freedom struggle took a new turn. Assassination of Englishmen, robberies and the severest punishment to the revolutionaries. Bombs exploded everywhere. The people supported the revolutionaries and kept them informed. A fresh wave of enthusiasm and excitement, prevailed. Congress condemned the violent incidents. This compelled the people to ignore even the Congress.

The main author of the revolutionary movement was Ganesh Damodar Savarkar. He distributed pamphlets which propagated the wiping out of all Englishmen from India. This led to the emergence of an armed organisation. Savarkar despatched a parcel of 20 Browning automatic pistols from Paris. The Magistrate of Nasik, Mr. Jackson handed over Savarkar to the Sessions and he was prosecuted for being a traitor. Jackson was struck with the first round of the fist pistol, and was killed. This incident gave further impetus to the freedom movement.

Meanwhile plans were also afoot to assassinate Curzon. Dhingra was to do it. However the plot failed. Dhingra was sentenced to death and hanged on 17 August, 1909. This accelerated the suppressive activities at India House in London and in Viceregal Lodge in India.

## Savarkar Imprisoned in the Andamans

The British Government sent spies after Savarkar. They had come to know that the pistol, which was fired to kill Jackson, had been sent by Savarkar. Savarkar was arrested for treason at Victoria Station. It was decided to send him to India.

Savarkar was being brought on board a ship to India. He escaped by jumping into the sea. The naval guards jumped after him but could not catch him. Savarkar swam and reached the harbour of Marseilles. From there he swam ashore. Now he was in an alien land, where he couldn't be arrested.

But the naval guards flouted all International Laws and arrested Savarkar. The French Government wrote to the British Government demanding the return of Savarkar. But the British Government paid no heed to it, and in the **Nasik Conspiracy Kand** (episode), Savarkar was sentenced to life imprisonment. He was thrown into the black cell of the Andamans. A lot of hue and cry was raised against it.

The masses were now full of anger and resentment. The whole country was under the grip of terrorist activities. The revolutionary activities were hastened by Sachindra Nath Sanyal of Benaras in U.P. Wachi Aiyar, in Madras shot down a magistrate which further boosted the morale of the revolutionaries. Neel Krishna Brahmchari and Shanker Krishna Aiyer imparted full vigour to the revolution.

## Lala Hardayal

The revolutionary groups abroad were also fully awake and vigilant. The Sikhs living in Canada and the USA who were often humiliated sided with the revolutionaries.

It was at this time that Lala Hardayal came forward, and he started thinking in terms of making Indians literate. He went to Oxford, for education, on Government scholarship, but when he found Indian students being dishonoured and ignored there, he abandoned the benefit of the scholarship and returned to India. English education and the British Government, as he thought, were both destructive to Indians, therefore, he left for San Francisco and motivated the Indians to work against the English. He collected 15,000 dollars and laid the foundation of the Indian Association. Later on this Association was renamed the Gadar (Mutiny) Party.

Lala Hardayal was arrested on his arrival to India. He was released on bail and he fled to Switzerland. He accelerated the revolutionary activities from there. Ras Behari Bose and Vishnu Ganesh came to Punjab. Removal of fish plates, making of bombs, calling Indians into one's fold, preparing flags and banners, cutting telegraph wires, collection of funds, gathering the rural groups and other such activities were planned. The Government detected all such activities and plans, and they began to arrest people on a large scale.. Five hundred people were prosecuted in Punjab, of whom five had to face court martial. 500 people were sentenced for life-imprisonment and sent to Cellular Jail in the Andamans.

Hardayal reached Japan and began to work there for the Indian Revolutionary Society. *Jahane-a-Islam* was published from Kustuntunia, and it also included articles in Arabic Urdu, Turkish and Hindi and in all of them there was a common message, "Kill the Englishmen. They are the enemies of independence." Thus, the revolutionaries kept the torch of independence burning either feebly or intensely. People at home and abroad came to know about the revolt of the Indians.

The British Government was completely shaken.

# 16

# Impact of the First World War on the Struggle for Independence

There was tension amongst the countries of Europe on account of several reasons. Imperialism was at its peak. Every country had began to consider herself supreme. It was at this time that the First World War broke out.

The Czars were ruling over Russia. Kaiser William ruled over Germany. Italy snatched away Turkey from the hands of Tripoli.

There was a secret alliance between France and Russia against Germany. A treaty was also signed between Belgium and England. When Germany launched a war against France, Russia also declared war against Germany. When Germany invaded Belgium, England also plunged into the war. At that very point Italy, America and Japan also joined the war. That was how the war assumed world-wide proportions.

The British Government now imposed a ban on Non-Resident Indians returning home. Germany instigated India for independence.

## Jahane-a-Islam

Amar Pasha made an appeal in *Jahane-a-Islam* to the Indians that it was high time that nearly 2 lakh English people were driven out of India. He excited thirty-two crores of Indians for violent actions.

The Congress, however, kept quiet after having reiterated and pressed their demand. The kings and Nawabs were busy attempting to prove their fidelity to the British. The Nawab of Hyderabad sent a telegram to the Governor General proving his fidelity. He instantly sent for two crore rupees. The kings and Nawabs were contemplating that by being helpful to the English people, they would be able to gain several benefits from them after the war. Madan Mohan Malviya said that if the English were defeated, it would create a crisis for them. Pheroz Shah Mehta was surrendering himself towards the English people. Even Lokmanya

Tilak was softening towards the government at that time. Gandhiji also felt that if the English won the war, they would give India its freedom.

When King George V came to India in 1911, he got the division of Bengal revoked and Bengal was made a province once again. Delhi was announced as the capital of India. This somewhat abated the wrath of the people. Everywhere spoke about the generosity of King George V.

## Home Rule Movement

Tilak propagated the idea of Home Rule Movement with full-fledged intensity. He declared that India as a nation wanted justice from the empire and that demand was based on the notion, "Freedom is our birth right".

This movement, however, remained confined only to the educated people. E.M. Montague became minister for India. He suggested that a responsible Government could only gradually be developed. This somewhat helped to calm the people.

The First World War was now over. It had involved an expenditure of one and a half arab pounds on the armed troops sent for the purpose. 9,53,374 Indian soldiers were sent, out of whom 5,000 Indian soldiers were missing 8,000 were imprisoned, 8,600 were wounded and 3,000 were killed.

On the other side Anne Besant was involved in intensifying the Home Rule Movement. She was a dauntless and courageous woman.

Britain and her allies were victorious in the First World War. Indians now began to wait for Britain to give her independence. They were fully confident that the British Government would certainly reward them in this manner in return for their loyalty.

## General O Dyer

It was a highly critical time. In 1917, eight lakh people died of plague. The prices were sky rocketing and labourers were still poorly paid. In the year 1918, the crops were altogether destroyed on account of famine. People were rendered jobless on account of recession. The Government adopted an adverse and suppressive attitude against the Home Rule Movement.

No body could have imagined the way the British Government would reward the sacrifices made by them during the war. The Government passed the Rowlatt

Act. This Act intended to crush the fundamental rights of the Indians, and consequently a country-wide strike was convened on 3rd March, 1919. Later on the date was shifted to 6th April. The information in regard to the change of date reached Delhi and other places late and the strike occurred there on the original date and the processions were also taken out.

The Government was bent upon exhibiting its force. There was firing in Delhi, in which 5 people were killed and several people wounded. Gandhiji was arrested. This news spread all over the country like wild fire.

Michael O Dyer was at that time the Lieutenant Governor of Punjab. He was strictly against political agitations. He even prohibited the entry of Congress leaders into Punjab. Hindus and Muslims were maintaining their unity in a perfect manner. This intimacy of the Hindus and Muslims angered the English.

The Congress workers of Punjab, Dr. Kichlu and Dr. Satya Pal, were sent to an unknown place. This incident added fuel to the fire.

The markets of Punjab immediately closed down. The citizens took out a huge procession for the liberation of their leaders. The procession went towards the residence of the District Magistrate. The police, however, halted the procession and began to fire indiscriminately at them. Consequently, ten people were killed and several others wounded.

The public of Amritsar got provoked at this brutal behaviour of the Government. The people grew violent. They carried the dead bodies and went around the city. On their way they killed any Englishman who came in the way. The crowd set fire to several buildings. That day as many as five Englishmen were killed.

## Jalianwalla Massacre

After this incident Michael O Dyer, handed over the town to the army.

The Hindu New Year commenced on 13 April, 1919. A public meeting was about to be held in the Jalianwalla Bagh. The meeting was scheduled at 4 pm. General Dyer announced that if meetings were held or processions dare taken out, or violent disturbances occurred, they would lead to disastrous consequences. Besides, he was also determined to teach the people a lesson so that in future they would dare not to hold meetings or take out processions.

20,000 people including men, women and children had gathered in the Jalianwalla Bagh surrounded by high walls from three sides. One side there was a narrow passage for getting inside and through which no gun-carriage could pass. The crowd, was quietly listening to their leader Hansraj.

At that very moment General Dyer, accompanied by 50 white men and a hundred other soldiers arrived there. It was nearly half past four.

General Dyer ordered the people in the crowd to disperse at once. They had no chance to think even for a moment. They merely saw the armed soldiers with their guns aiming towards the crowd. Dyer had blocked their passage. There was a well, three trees and a tomb and that was all there in the name of a garden in Jalianwalla Bagh.

"Fire !" ordered General Dyer. The crowd attempted to run hither and thither, but there was no way for them to get out. There was only one narrow passage to go out but that too was blocked by General Dyer.

Amidst shrieks and shouts, children, men and women were indiscriminately shot. Within the twinkling of an eye, four hundred people were killed and over 2,000 were wounded. There were 1,600 rounds of fire, which was the total stock in their possession.

Dyer was still not appeased. He ordered that martial law be clamped at once and issued strict orders for its compliance. It was announced that those who flouted the orders in any manner, would be punished heavily.

In Amritsar, there was a total black-out and water supply was also cut off. Cycles were snatched and people were compelled to creep with their chests rubbing against the rough ground. Brutal treatment was given to wayfarers. The prices of articles in the shops were fixed as per the orders of the soldiers. The Indians were ordered to salute the whites. The issue of third class tickets at the Railway Stations was stopped.

## Free Langars (Meals)

People had to endure inhuman atrocities at several places viz. Chutiarkhana, Jalalpur, Sheikhpura, Layalpur, Jatt etc. on account of martial law. Hunger was rampant in Punjab and people were dying of starvation. Har Krishan Lal grew restless and opened free *langars* in Lahore. The Government was so displeased and annoyed that his property worth 90 lakhs was confiscated and he was sentenced to the Andamans (Kala Pani).

## Hunter Commission

Dyer's misdeeds were condemned everywhere, at home as well as abroad. The great poet Rabindra Nath Tagore renounced the title of "sir". An inquiry commission was set up under the chairmanship of Lord Hunter. It was just an eyewash, a device to conceal the facts. In the report of Hunter's Commission, the action of General Dyer was justified, but the methods were considered somewhat improper.

Congress also set up a Commission under the chairmanship of Gandhiji, by which the so called 'noble' intentions of the British Government were exposed.

17

# The Last Phase Under Gandhiji

## Non-Cooperation Movement

The suppressive policies of the Government had now become unbearable. The president of the Muslim League, Jinnah warned the Government. Gandhiji passed the resolution of Non-Cooperation. Tilak died on 1 August, 1920, on the same day the Non-Cooperation Movement was launched. The resolution of Gandhiji was strongly opposed. Moti Lal Nehru and the Ali brothers specially supported his resolution. Gandhiji in a memorable lecture reiterated in powerful words :

"The British Government plays the devil. It is impossible to co-operate with it."

The English were quite apprehensive about this resolution. Gandhiji had already enjoyed special fame and prestige with his programme of truth and non-violence in South Africa. The resolution, which had not been passed, was tabled once again after a year and it was passed by a majority.

The Non-Cooperation Movement soon spread to other parts of India.

To begin with, Gandhiji returned the Gold Medal given to him by the British to him, to the Governor General. The students left Government schools and colleges and sought admission to National institutions. Advocates abandoned their practice. Lala Lajpat Rai in Punjab, Rajendra Prasad in Bihar, Vallabh Bhai Patel in Gujarat, Moti Lal Nehru and Jawahar Lal Nehru in Uttar Pradesh, Raj Gopalachari in Madras, Chittaranjan Das in Bengal and several others renounced their legal practice. Maulana Mohammad Ali, Shaukat Ali, Maulana Abul Kalam Azad, Dr. Ansari and others boycotted the courts. The All India Congress Committee had a three-point agenda to be accomplished within three months.

(*i*) to collect Rupees one crore to as funds,

(*ii*) to enroll one crore people as members of the Congress; and

(*iii*) to bring 20 lakh *charkhas* (spinning wheels) into operation.

Foreign articles were set on fire. Foreign hats, collars, ties, suits, dolls, were all thrown into the fire. The movement was in full swing.

The triumphant chants of 'Vande Mataram' and 'Allah-o-Akbar' could be heard from all directions.

Gandhiji explained to all,

"Our enemy is strong. Hence, it will be a prolonged struggle. It you think of participating in it, you must be prepared to sacrifice everything. You must strictly adhere to the norms of non-violence and discipline".

The world was curiously looking on at the turn of events in India. Every worker felt the impact of Gandhiji's words deep down in his heart.

The plight of the state governments was worse. The citizens hardly enjoyed any priviledge. There was neither any newspaper, nor an independent municipality. Even Indian States People's Councils (*Praja Parishad*) were obliged to hold their meetings in British India. They were not allowed to convene meetings in the states. The states were internally perturbed about the impetuous lovers of independence. They didn't even want that the spark of the activities of independence should at all reach them, and flare up into a rebellion against them. Indigenous states were vigilant about the Non-Cooperation Movement. They felt upset with the increasing influence of Gandhiji and the activities of the Congress tormented them.

# 18 The Revolutionaries Unstable the British

## Mopla Revolution

The wave of the Non-Cooperation Movement soon touched the Malabar Coast in the far South. The Arabs settled there in the 9th century had got married to Dravidian women. Their descendants came to be known as Moplas. Violent and brave by nature, they soon started collecting arms and weapons. When the local administration detected their secret planning, the police came to search them. It gave rise to riots. The rioters surrounded the police at Pukkotar, and at Parghanangi. Violent and destructive activities broke out. An English military officer was assassinated, the railway station was destroyed and fish plates were removed.

The British troops were defeated at different points. Meanwhile, Mohammad Hazi declared himself King. The English people called in the Gurkhas, and armed forces from Garhwal and Cochin. At last, the Moplas had to surrender. More than 2,000 Moplas were killed, and 6,000 were captured. A court martial was ordered for the King and his followers, and the remaining were sentenced to long-term imprisonment.

The English resorted to abominable conspiracies to avenge themselves against the Moplas. About 100 Moplas were picked up and packed into the coach of a goods train. The iron sheets and the iron walls of the coach got extremely heated, and consequently at Podanur station, when the coach was unlocked 68 imprisoned Moplas were found dead.

The Moplas were opposed to Hindus. They were not directly linked with the Non-Cooperation Movement but they wanted to derive benefit out of it, and wanted to lay the foundation of a Muslim empire, but their dreams couldn't be realized.

The Mopla agitation cooled down. In fact, it wasn't a revolution, but a riot, a personified madness.

## Chauri-Chaura Episode

The Non-Cooperation Movement was achieving success at different levels. The British Government was internally perturbed. Meanwhile, at Chauri-Chaura an incident occurred. The crowd set fire to the Chauri-Chaura station house. Consequently, a sub-inspector, and 21 constables were burnt to death in that fire. On account of this very reason, this movement was withdrawn by Gandhiji. He believed that non-violence didn't go deep down into the hearts of the people. Ironically, when Gandhiji announced the discontinuance of this movement, he was arrested by the British Government.

By withdrawing this movement, Gandhiji shattered the hopes of the Indian people. Many contend that Gandhiji did a blunder in withdrawing the Non-Cooperation Movement. C.F. Andrews, however, wrote : Subhash Chandra Bose called it nothing short of National misfortune when public enthusiasm was at its climax. Gandhiji was accused of treachery for his articles published in *Young India* and he was sentenced to 6 years imprisonment.

## Kakori Episode

There were quite a few people who didn't participate in the Non-Cooperation Movement. There was also a few who were bent upon throwing off the British yoke. Among them was Ram Prasad, who absconded from the Mainpuri conspiracy. Yogesh Chandra Chatterji was then the leader of the Revolutionary Group. Ashfaq Ulla Khan had also joined that group. Rajendra Lahidi was a person with revolutionary ideology, and was an active member of that group.. Chandra Shekhar Azad was also frustrated by the withdrawal of the Non-Cooperation Movement by the revolutionary group.

Azad was one of those boys who was arrested during the Non-Cooperation Movement and against whom an inquiry was made. When Azad was asked his name, his father's name and such other particulars, he declared :

“Azad is my name. ‘*Swadheen*’ (independent) is my father’s name, and ‘Prison’ is my residence.” He bluntly told the Magistrate. ‘In a maladministration and misrule ‘Prison’ is the only abode for free people.”

By the order of the Magistrate he was punished by 15 lashes. With every stroke of the stick Azad shouted : “Long Live Mahatma Gandhi !”

To continue with their activities the revolutionaries required a lot of money. In 1925, at Kakori near Lucknow, the incident of robbing the railway treasury occurred. Azad was involved in it. The treasury was being despatched by the Eight Down train. The robbery was planned by Pandit Ram Prasad, but Ashfaq Ulla Khan was against this action. But then how could the arms and weapons needed by the revolutionaries be brought ? It was decided that somewhere near Kakori the train must be detained by pulling the chain, and the bags containing money must be stolen.

Besides Azad, several others revolutionaries such as Rajendra Nath Lahiri, Ram Prasad ‘Bismil’, Ashfaq Ulla Khan, Roshan Singh, Manmath Nath Gupta, Mukund Lal Keshav, Sachindra Nath Bakshi, Banwari Lal etc. were involved it. These people collected chisels, sledge-hammers and hammers and boarded the Eight down train from Shahjahanpur. Armed men were keeping watch on the

trunk containing the money. For this specific work Rajendra Nath Lahidi, Sachindra Nath Bakshi and Ashfaq Ulla Khan were chosen. They were all in a second class compartment, and the remaining were in a third class compartment. Ram Prasad was the leader. Four of them were equipped with Mauser pistols. Each pistol was loaded with fifty rounds.

As planned, Rajendra Nath pulled the chain. The train halted after some time. The setting sun was about to mark the closing of the day. The guard got down in search of the coach where the chain was pulled. The other passengers also got down. Ram Prasad pointing his pistol at the guard ordered him to lie on the ground with his face facing downwards. Meanwhile the other revolutionaries forced themselves into the compartment which contained the treasure box, and threw out the treasure box. But no one had the key of that box. Even the guard didn't have it. With great difficulty only a small hole in the box could be made. Ashfaq Ulla Khan handed over the pistol to Manmath Nath, and himself started to widen the hole till it was possible to take out the money.

Several rounds were fired in the air. All were warned not to get down from the train. Those who had got down boarded the train again. Indian armed soldiers sat in the train quietly. They didn't pick up the rifles in reply. The White Major, an Englishman, didn't come out of his coach.

It was all over within 10 minutes. One passenger was killed. The revolutionaries got down and escaped into the jungle. 40 passengers were arrested.

It was a prestigious case for the government and they spent 10 lakh rupees on it. Pandit Jagat Narayan Mulla was the public prosecutor. He was paid five hundred rupees per day. Govind Vallabh Pant and Chandra Bhanu and others were fighting the case on behalf of the accused. The case went on for eighteen months. Sachindra Nath was sentenced to the Black Waters. Manmath Nath Gupta was sentenced to 14 years imprisonment, and Pandit Ram Prasad 'Bismil', Roshan Singh, Rajendra Nath Lahidi and Ashfaq Ulla Khan were sentenced to death.

An appeal signed by the members of the Central Assembly was made to the Lord Lieutenant. The death sentence was postponed twice, but the government was bent upon hanging them.

Rajendra Nath Lahiri was hanged on 19th December, 1927.

"I am well prepared for what is going to happen on 19th December. What is death after all, except the transference from one body to another. I believe that my soul will quickly come back with new vigour and vitality and be in action for the liberation of my motherland and my people". It was also accompanied by a poem :

"Even if I have to die a thousand times
for my country,
I may never feel the pangs of it,
Oh ! God ! I may be born in India a
hundred times,
And every time action for the benefit
of my country
Should be the motive of my death.
Bismil, Rosha. Lahidi, Ashfaq die
of oppressions
Hundred of patriots will crop up
Out of the drops of their blood.
Their incessant endeavours would
redeem the country and end once and for all
Our innumerable griefs and sorrows
Good Bye to all."
"While he was ready to be hanged, his last utterance was,
"O God ! May Your Will Prevail
May You and You alone
Live for ever
I may be no more,
My desire shall be no more
So long, as there is breath in me
And blood in my veins
May Your Name be on my lips
And May Your Will Prevail."

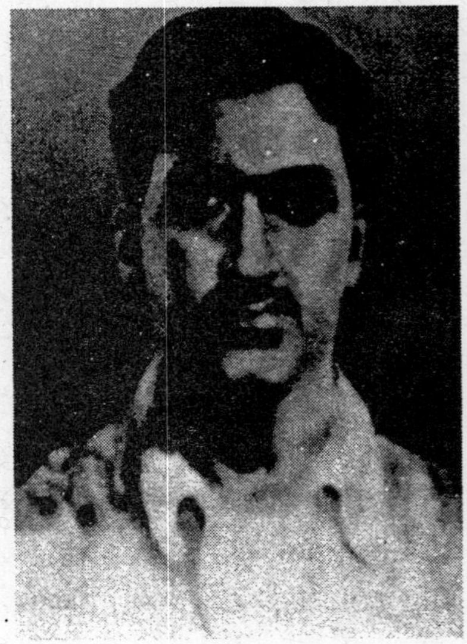

He chanted 'Vande Matram' three times and thrice he chanted 'Long Live Mother India.' When he was about to be hanged, he said, "I want that the British Empire must be wiped out."

With 'Vande Matram' on his lips, he went to the scaffold. At Gorakhpur it was a historic procession, in which his dead body was taken.

On 19th December itself **Ashfaq Ulla Khan** was hanged.

"Having felt fully annoyed with
their limitless tortures

I, a descendant of Adam say
Good bye to Faizabad."

He came close to the hanging place and kissed it.

"I have never shed human blood to cover my hands with
The allegation against me is altogether wrong.
Justice will be delivered in the land of God."

He remembered God and became a martyr.

**Roshan Singh** was also sentenced to death and on 19th December he was hanged in Allahabad jail. He, too, went to the scaffold chanting 'Vande Mataram'.

After Kakori case the revolutionaries were scattered till Chandra Shekhar Azad reorganised them again. One again the revolutionary group was organized and it included Sukhdev, Yash Pal, Fanindra Nath Ghosh, Bhagat Singh, Kundan Lal, Vijay Kumar Singh, Brahm Datta, Surendra Nath Pandey and others. Those people made several efforts to get the Kakori prisoners released, but they could not succeed. Azad now led the revolutionaries. It started making bombs in Lahore, Agra, Calcutta and other places secretly.

## Boycott of Simon Commission

In 1928, a commission came to India under the chairmanship of Sir John Simon. The commission was named after him, and came to decide the destiny of India. However, the people protested vehemently shouting slogans of 'Go back Simon ! Go back Simon !" A large procession was taken out. The police lathi-charged the procession. Even Lala Lajpat Rai couldn't escape the strokes of the police lathis. He was seriously wounded and succumbed to his injuries soon after.

## Saunders' Assassination

Several members of the revolutionary group were part of the procession. They solemnly pledged to avenge the death of Lala Lajpat Rai. It was decided that the officer responsible for his assassination must first be killed. On 15th December, when Saunders was coming on his motor-cycle, Shivram Raj and Bhagat Singh fired at him. Saunders died on the spot. The British government was taken by surprise. Bhagat Singh got himself clean-shave and accompanied by Raj Guru, they left Lahore by train posing as pilgrims.

The revolutionary group came to be known by its new name 'Indian Socialist Democratic Army'.

Their slogans were :

"Imperialism : Be doomed and destroyed".

"Revolution : Long live ! Long live !"

## Bomb Explosion in Delhi Assembly

The revolutionaries now decided to explode a bomb in Delhi Assembly so as to awaken the deaf and blind government. Bhagat Singh was entrusted with this job.

It was planned that Bhagat Singh and Batukeshwar would drop the bomb in the assembly and Azad and others would save them and bring them back safely. But Bhagat Singh did not fear arrest or death.

On 8th April, 1929 while a strong debate was going on the floor of the Assembly, suddenly a bomb went off with a loud explosion and smoke spread everywhere.

Bhagat Singh and Batukeshwar Dutt appeared there and shouted :

"Imperialism : be doomed and destroyed."

"Revolution : Long live ! Long live !"

They also threw a piece of paper, on which it was written, "The explosion is necessary to make the deaf hear."

Half an hour later they were arrested. On 7th October, 1930 Bhagat Singh, Raj Guru and Sukhdev were sentenced to death. The entire country stood up in protest against this judgement.

Bhagat Singh, before becoming a martyr, wrote in a letter to his brother :

Dear Kulttar,

I was sorry to see tears in your eyes today. What all you said today was full of deep pathos. Your tears are beyond my endurance. Dear, be bold and acquire full education. Take care of your physique, be courageous and genial with all around you. What else shall I say ...?

His worry is to evolve : what
could be a new mode of
oppression every time ?
We are fond of seeing : what
could be the last limit
of tortures?
Why should we get annoyed at home ?
Why should we complain of expenditure ?

Let us face the eventuality,
even if the whole world
goes against us.
I am just a quest to some moment,
in the flux of time
In the theatre of this world
I am a burning lamp in the morn
About to be damped,
The breeze that touches me
Blows with a lightening thought
In the midst of glorious uncertainties
do we live
Out of the dust we emerge
And into the dust shall we
mingle again
Well I beg leave of you
Good Bye my countrymen, be happy
We are in the course of
A LONG PILGRIMAGE
Live with zest and lie with cheers !
Adieu ! Adieu ! Adieu !

Your brother,

BHAGAT SINGH

The next plan of the revolutionaries was to blow up the Viceroy's train. The Viceroy was travelling from Kolhapur to Delhi. Bombs were put under the rails. These bombs were connected to an electric battery, placed at a distance of 100 yards. However, the plan failed because the wire was to be drawn the moment the Viceroy's coach was over the bombs. However, it was late by a few seconds, and consequently the Viceroy's coach remained unaffected but its adjoining compartment blew up.

Congress leaders condemned the episode, though the public welcomed it.

The Government now arrested the revolutionaries one by one. Bhagwati Charan was killed while carrying a bomb. The bomb exploded on the way. Jagdish died in a police encounter at Shalimar Garden in Lahore. The Government was bent upon crushing the revolutionaries.

# 19 India Towards Complete Independence

People were favourably inclined towards the revolutionaries. Congress was confronted with a state of indecision. It couldn't ascertain what to do.

For the Congress Session of 1929 as many as 3 nominations were received for presidentship. Gandhiji received 10 votes, Patel 5 and Jawaharlal Nehru 3. Gandhiji withdrew his name, and as advised by him, Patel also withdrew. Consequently, Nehru became the President of the session.

## Full Independence

The Congress session was held under the presidentship of Jawaharlal Nehru in Lahore from 25th December to 31st December, in the year 1929.

On 31st December, exactly a minute after midnight, full freedom (*Purna Swarajya*) was announced as the final aim. The session was held on the bank of the river Ravi, where all the people were filled with joy and excitement. Nehru said : "We are in favour of full independence for India. Congress doesn't accept that we should be any more governed by the ordinances of the British Government."

On this occasion Pandit Nehru was welcomed in grand manner. A huge procession led by Gandhiji, Patel, Subhas Chandra Bose and others was taken out. It was also decided at that time that 26th January should be celebrated as a day of absolute independence.

## Dandi March

The movement had to be accelerated and the wave of change had to be felt. Subhas Chandra Bose was abroad at that time. Gandhiji had already sought the approval from Congress for the salt agitation. Subash Chandra Bose wanted the changes in the Congress in regard to policy, manner, and methods. What they all needed was intensity.

The Dandi March was a kind of experiment — to exhibit the strength of non-violence and bring about a new consciousness in the people. Gandhiji in a letter written to the Viceroy, clearly explained his policy. Now there was hardly anything secret.

On 12th March, 1930, Gandhiji along with 70 companions launched his journey on foot from Sabarmati to Dandi. Gandhiji wanted to remove fear from the mind of people by violating the salt law and also wanted the people to realize the invincible power of the soul.

Gandhiji wore just a loin cloth and dhoti and a sheet to cover his shoulders, and just behind him were 79 followers in rows of two. All the people offered *arti.*

Gandhiji was in the fore front and just behind him were the *Satyagrahis* who were being followed by innumerable crowds of Indian people. The grand procession taken was unprecedented in the history of Ahmedabad. The whole city seemed to have joined the procession, which was about 2 miles long. The atmosphere was resounding with frequent shouts of—"Long Live Gandhiji !"

Gandhiji said on this occasion : "If independence is not achieved, I shall either die on the way, or reside outside the Ashram. If I am not able to get the salt-law abrogated, I shall have no intention of going back to the Ashram at all."

Gandhiji announced that no Satyagraha would be launched until he reached Dandi. The Satyagrahis sang invocation songs during *Prabhat pheris* (morning rounds). "It is morning now, traveller ! What makes you sleep, while the night is past."

The flag song also became most popular with them.

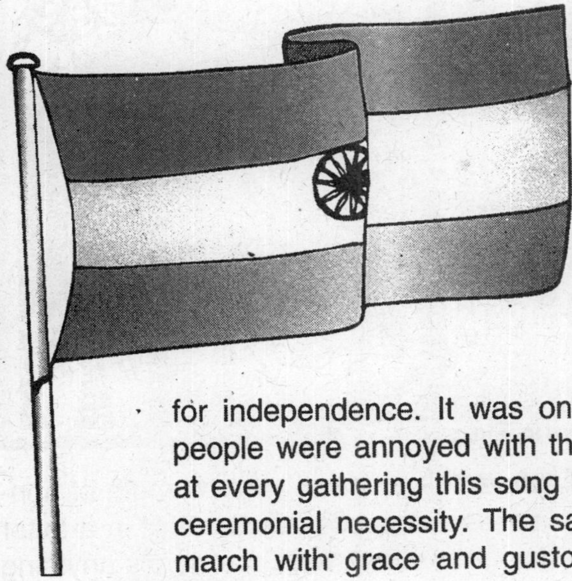

On 13th April 1924, in Phoolbag of Kanpur, Jalianwalla Bagh day was celebrated. For the first time Shyam Lal Gupta Parshad (Councillor) composed a Flag Song, which was sung by Jawaharlal Nehru and all those who were present there. Parshad was inspired by Ganesh Shanker Vidyarthi to compose the Flag Song, and in 1925 it was published in *Pratap*. The song became the soul force of the struggle for independence. It was on the lips of one and all. The English people were annoyed with the Flag Song. In every procession and at every gathering this song had to be sung as a conventional and ceremonial necessity. The same song was sung during the Dandi march with grace and gusto. The text of the Flag Song runs as under :

"Our dear lovely tricolour
With its victory over the World
Our Flag Must Always Fly High
Our Flag is a perennial fountain of strength for us
It brings joy and gaiety to the brave
Our Flag is the body and soul of our Motherland
Our Flag Must Always Fly High in the fierce struggle for freedom
Moment by moment
We shall see it and feel excited
The enemy will see it, and
begin to tremble in their minds
Our fear and crisis must be on
the vanishing point
Our Flag Must Always Fly High
Under the Shelter of this flag
We shall firmly determine to achieve independence
Long Live Bharat Mata

Long Live Mother India
Independence is our aim
Our Sole Objective
Our flag Must Always Fly High
Come ! My dear brave patriots, come
With a spirit of sacrifices,
For our country and her faith
Let us get together and sing
India is our dear country
Our Flag Must Always Fly High
We shall sacrifice ourselves
But shall never bear a scratch
To the honour and dignity of our Flag
We shall achieve victory over the world
And then only
Our pledge shall be fulfilled
Our dear lovely tricolour
Our flag Must Always Fly High."

Under the leadership of Gandhiji this group of people were marching towards Dandi. This journey was to be completed in 24 days. Sardar Patel was informing people well in advance about Gandhiji's arrival, but the Government meanwhile arrested him. Nevertheless the peasants and villagers were well informed about Gandhiji's arrival. Gandhiji strongly wished that they must reach Dandi on 5th April and on 6th April itself, on Jalianwalla Bagh Massacre Day, they must break the salt-law.

Village after village were pouring in. Day by day the enthusiasm of the people was swelling like the sea tide. Gandhiji reached the sea shore at the scheduled hour, and from there he picked up a handful of salt. The atmosphere began to resound with jubilant shouts of 'Long Live the great Gandhi Baba.'

Gandhiji said : "The Salt Law has systematically been broken. Now everybody is free to prepare salt anywhere according to convenience at the risk of a legal penalty. I advise that workers must prepare salt everywhere."

Fearlessness and courage motivated people to prepare salt.

On 4th May Gandhiji was sleeping at Karadi tent. The English Magistrate from Surat, accompanied by 30 armed constables surrounded the tents at Karadi. The Magistrate read out the orders :

"Since the Governor General in Council considers the activities of Mohandas Karamchand Gandhi as dangerous and hence issues orders that the said Mohandas Karamchand Gandhi is, in accordance with the provisions of the clause 35 of the Regulation of 1827, under strict restrictions and he must be under arrest as long as the Government desires."

Gandhiji handed over the leadership to Smt. Sarojini Naidu and was sent to Yervada Jail. Gandhiji's arrest by the British Government added fuel to fire. It awakened the whole country. Workers staged demonstrations in Mumbai, shopkeepers closed down their shops. In Gujarat no rent was paid. The markets all over the country were closed.

At last the Government surrendered and came to a compromise with the people. Satyagrahis were released. The properties, forfeited earlier, were returned to their respective owners and the Government employees were taken back in service.

## The Last Day of Azad

For 10 years the British Government could not rest, because Chandrashekar Azad created such a hullabaloo during that span.

It was nearly 10 in the morning on 27th February, 1931. Azad was in Allahabad. He had his eye on Veer Bhadra Tewari. He felt mentally upset. Veer Bhadra had been arrested in the Kakori Kand episode but he was released. Why?

Azad was sitting with his friend Sukhdev Raj in the Alfred Park of Allahabad. The police officer Visesar Singh spotted Azad with his sharp eyesight. He intimated the Superintendent of Police Naut Bower, who rushed at once to the spot in his jeep.

The late Prime Minister Indira Gandhi who was an eye witness to the whole thing said about that event : "I think I wasn't able to see the last rounds of fire. I just saw fire coming out of the gun, and heard the gunshots. I saw all this from my house, and was stunned, as if someone had thrown me into very hot or very cold water."

Naut Bower halted the jeep at a distance of 10 yards and said :

"Azad, you are surrounded from all sides. Surrender yourself."

Azad signalled to Sukhdev Raj to escape. Sukhdev Raj was hiding behind a tree. He left through the rear. The police kept a vigilant eye on Azad. Azad felt that it was his last day. He smiled and said :-

"Mr. Bower ! Azad is born for FREEDOM, and certainly not for surrender."

Naut Bower had not fired till then. Now his bullet pierced through the thigh of Azad. Azad in return fired at Bower, whose wrist was pierced. His pistol dropped from his hand and fell some distance away, and he just managed to save his life by standing behind a tree.

Azad had plenty of cartridges left. But how long could he continue to fight ? He had sustained severe wounds and he collapsed and died.

The government didn't give Azad's dead body to the people, but the people began to worship that tree near which his martyrdom occurred. The government was provoked and consequently the tree was cut down from there.

# 20

# Netaji Calls out— "Dilli Chalo"

The Second World War had begun. The British Government was bent upon plunging India into the World War. Indians were being recruited into the army under compulsion. People revolted against it.

## Subhash Chandra Bose Arrested

On 6th April, 1940 the Civil Disobedience Movement was launched and Subhash Chandra Bose thought that if India worked against Britain by joining hands with her opponents, she could achieve independence. What was he to do then ? He wanted to find out a way to escape and come out of prison.

He went on a fast to protest against the attitude of the government. The government released him, but he was kept under strict vigilance.

## Subhash Disappears

On 17th January, 1941 Subhash hoodwinked the government and disguised as a Khilji Pathan, escaped from his house. He went to Berlin via Kabul and Russia.

He met Hitler, but Hitler gave him no assurance of independence, and Subhash became frustrated. Japan was trampling East Asia and had defeated the British Army in Malaya. The defeat of the British Army showed him one way out. The Army consisting only of Indian prisoners of war were handed over to Captain Mohan Singh, who was in the British Army.

## Indian National Army

The Indian National Army consisted only of the prisoners of war. A division was made of 16,000 soldiers. Subhash wanted to recruit 40,000 prisoners of war into the army, but the Japanese Government didn't permit him to do so. At last, he was taken into custody. The future of the Indian National Army was now in the midst of uncertainties. Subhash at that time was invited to become the leader. Subhash started from Keel Port and reached Tokyo by submarine and plane, where he met the Prime Minister, Tozo. Tozo declared in the Japanese Diet (Parliament) that he would fully help India in the task of achieving independence.

Subhash came from Japan to Singapore and there he formed an adhoc Government of independent India and took the Salute of the Indian National Army. He said : "This is our last effort towards independence. In this process you may have to endure hunger, pain, long expeditions and even death. If you succeed in your endeavours, you will certainly achieve independence."

Subhash became the President, Prime Minister, and the Supreme Commander of the adhoc Government. M.C. Chatterjee became Finance Minister, S.A. Aiyyer became Publicity Minister and Luxmi Swaminathan became Minister for Women's Organisation.

First of all Subhash took the pledge :

"I take this solemn pledge in the name of God that I shall liberate 38 crores of Indian People. I, Subhash Chandra Bose, shall continue to fight this sacred war of independence till my last breath."

The government was recognized by six nations including Japan, Italy and Germany.

The war began, and it brought a new ray of hope to India. The British Government was perturbed a great deal.

## March to Delhi

Before leaving Rangoon for Aracon, Subhash, said : Comrades, my soldiers ! The slogan of your was will be, "March to Delhi ! (Dilli Chalo)"

The Indian National Army, after defeating the British troops, entered India at-Maddock. Kahiya was snatched and the tricolour was hoisted. The Indian National Army had only rifles and machine guns. They had no aircrafts, no garrison, and no medical facilities. Nevertheless, Subhash Bose was telling his soldiers to keep up their morale :

"Soldiers of India ! Far beyond, across the rivers and mountain peaks, is our motherland, where we were born and in whose lap we shall return now."

"Can't you listen ? Your motherland is calling you. 38 crores of Indian people are calling you. Blood is calling blood. Awake ! We have no time to lose ! Take up your arms. The way to Delhi is the way to independence. March to Delhi."

The Army marched ahead. They entered the land of India. But Japan was losing ground. Subhash was going from Singapore to Tokyo. When the plane took off from Tahihock airport in the afternoon at two, one of the propellors of its engine broke. Within the twinkling of an eye the plane crashed and fell down on the ground. The petrol tank caught fire.

"When Subhash came out of the plane, he was terribly burnt. His clothes had caught fire and he was taken to hospital, but couldn't be saved. At nine at night he died. His dream could't be realized but the British Government was completely upset. They began to think that it would be impossible to keep India suppressed henceforth.

# 21

# India Achieves Independence

In the Second World War Britain was getting weaker and weaker. There was internal conflict even within Congress, but Congress wanted that if Britain assured India of her independence, they would help. What did India gain when she helped Britain during the First World War ? How easily Britain had broken away from her assurance ? Britain was ready to grant colonial independence to India, but Congress now expected full and absolute independence.

Gandhiji made an appeal that India should help Britain.

## Full (absolute) Independence

At Ramgarh, Bihar Congress had its session on 19th and 20th March, 1940, in which the President Maulana Abul Kalam Azad said :

"The country is passing through a period of crisis. We must forget all distinctions and discriminations and get united. Full independence is the aim of Congress."

Leaflets were being distributed :

NOT A PENNY : No penny will be contributed towards the war.

NOT A BROTHER : No person will be allowed to be recruited to the Army.

NOT AN ARTICLE : No supply of articles and material would be made for the army.

When Gandhiji delivered a speech at Pavnar, he and Congress President Maulana Abul Kalam Azad were sent to prison. Gandhiji realized that people were not interested in being sent to prison. He said :

"I am not going to prison this time on my own. In this struggle there is hardly any point in courting arrest. Going to prison by your own choice will be a very mild step. So long we have indulged in the action of courting arrest. This time my intention is that the Movement should gain intensity in the right way."

## Quit India Movement

On 23rd March, 1942 Sir Stanford Cripps came to India. He was a lover of justice, freedom and liberty. Britain started releasing the imprisoned leaders to gain India's sympathy. America also was sympathetic to India.

Cripps didn't succeed in his tricks of rhetoric to entrap Indian leaders, because they were all supporters of full independence. It was very clearly visible that Britain was not able to protect India. Japan had already captured Burma, Malaya and Singapore. Japan was fighting the war not against India, but against Britain.

Gandhiji was perhaps in search for such an opportunity. He was prepared to give leadership to the simmering sentiments of the people. Subhash Chandra Bose was able to attract people all the more. Gandhiji advised the British people to quit India. If they did not do that, they would have to face the wrath of the whole of India.

## Do or Die

The scenario was fast changing. On 9th August, 1942 at 10 at night on the Gwalior Tank Ground of Bombay, Gandhiji while addressing a meeting, said :

"Achieve Independence do or die"

This message, like the rays of the newly rising sun spread all over India on the morning of 10th August, 1942. On the same day Gandhiji, Nehru, Abdul Kalam Azad, Rajendra Prasad and others were arrested. On 10th August the atrocities of the government became the cruelest. Patel announced that within a week India would achieve independence. Consequently, the people were out for open revolt. In their anger and fury they destroyed railway stations, invaded post offices and cut telegraph wires, burnt police stations, and dismantled the government buildings.

Workers went on strike. The mills in Gujarat were closed down. The army destroyed thousands of houses and killed hundreds of people. At Hazipur the crowds invaded a prison house and liberated nearly a thousand prisoners. The Superintendent of Madhuvani Jail was arrested. All the prisoners except the *satyagrahis* ran away from prison.

Dr. Lohia was put to new kinds of torture by the Government. He was kept awake round the clock. Jai Prakash Narayan went on hunger strike in prison. His hunger strike went on for 31 days.

In this Movement about 15,000 people were killed and one and a half lakh people were wounded. A lot of property was destroyed.

On the other side, the Indian National Army, under the leadership of Subhash Bose was marching towards Delhi. That created a new excitement among the people. From all sides only two voices could be heard : 'Quit India' and 'March to Delhi'.

Meanwhile, America dropped the atom bomb on Japan, Germany, Italy etc. were defeated, but this victory proved to be very costly to the allied nations. They couldn't henceforth keep India under their control, since they were themselves exhausted.

## Towards Independence

In 1945, Churchill was defeated in the elections and the Labour Party won. The British Prime Minister, Atlee announced that 3 members of the Cabinet must study the political impact of India and advise if India was to be given independence.

## First day of Independence

Numerous acts of arson followed people were killed; they lost their houses and belonging and were won't to wander aimless.

Hindus and Muslims at times were bent upon killing each other. From one end there was a slogan "Har Har Mahadev", which was replied from the other end, "Allah-o-Akbar". Those people often came out in groups with naked swords in their hands to kill one another.

"Independence is my birth right." Whether there be Pakistan or Hindustan, we must have our birth right. Remember, that those powers, which you have left behind, will work for you. Air, earth, ether — every breath of air will not forget you. You have several companions, several friends, such as enthusiasm and worship; love and the invincible human heart."

Most of the people who participated in the decisive meeting of the All India Congress Committee on 15th June 1947, were in favour of Partition. Sardar Vallabh Bhai Patel said :

"If a finger gets poisoned, it should be removed lest it affects the whole body."

Pandit Nehru was also of the same opinion. All wanted independence, even at the cost of Partition. Gandhiji never wanted it. He declared, 'If at all there be Partition, it would be over my dead body'.

Hindustan and Pakistan, however, came into being during his lifetime only. He was a silent spectator to it.

Dr. Ram Monohar Lohia did make some desperate efforts but the Congress leaders, were afraid that they should not miss what they were about to gain. Later on Dr. Lohia said. "Partition was the child of a feeble crumbling leadership in the torturing circumstances."

Nehru hardly had any alternative left. Besides, he was also completely tied. Thirdly, the destruction of innocent lives and material in the communal riots occurring almost everyday frightened him. If partition brought an end to violence and bloodshed, and led to free and peaceful life, it would be much better.

And Partition occurred.

On 14th August, 1947, Pakistan came into being, and on 15th August, 1947, at mid-night India achieved Independence.

## Celebrations on 15th August 1947

Darbar Hall, 15th August, 1947. It was nearly half-past eight in the morning. The trumpets blew. Lord Mountbatten, wearing a red and golden apparel entered accompanied by Mrs. Mountbatten.

The celebrations of Independence began. Lord Mountbatten took an oath of the office of Governor General. He said : "I may be considered as one among you, who has been fully committed to promote the interests of the country."

His speech was applauded everywhere. Dr. Rajendra Prasad responded to his speech first in Hindi and then in English.

"The British rule over India comes to an end today. Now our relations with Britain will be based on equality, good wishes and mutual benefit."

Thereafter, on the Council House, the National tricolour with its saffron, white and green shades began to wave in the air and was honoured with a 31 gun salute.

## Salute to the Flag in Princess Park

From there they all came to Princess Park. The programme of saluting to the Flag began near the War Memorial. The function and ceremonies were witnessed by three lakh people. All faces were beaming with geniality, fervour and furore. It seemed that the sea of people would very soon submerge that small island. All were present there but Gandhiji was conspicuous by his absence.

Everywhere the people were in a state of joy, gaiety and ecstasy. The country had achieved independence. All were in jubilant spirits. As the Flag was being hoisted, it began to drizzle. It was a memorable day with lots of thrills and romantic moments.

Though the mood was jubilant Maha Yogi Arvind was apprehensive. He said in his message:

"India is independent today, but she has yet not achieved unity".

Hindus and Muslims were not mentally united. He was an optimist and expected that the fact of partition was not to be established once and for all. It might be considered as a terminal requirement. If the partition continued, it would cause some serious weaknesses and disabilities and it could also give rise to a situation of internal conflict.' He said at last :'

"In whatever way it is possible Partition must come to an end."

Our first Prime Minister Pandit Jawaharlal Nehru said : "In the mid-night hour, while the whole world is asleep, India will awake in the new heaven of freedom. The future is not easy, nor is it meant for comforts. It is meant for constant hard work, and only then shall we be able to fulfil all those promises which we have made so far and which we are going to make today itself. We are representatives of India and appeal to the people of India that they must cooperate with us in this great task."

"Thus, India achieved independence. The country was divided into two parts. Gandhiji was stuck with this grief that though the country did become independent, yet it was divided. Lakhs of people lost their houses or were killed.

We achieved independence on the strength of the non-violence of Mahatma Gandhi. But the celebrations of independence were covered with blood-shed, as if we all had gone mad. We were cutting each other's throats, burning houses and looting property. It was indeed a matter of regret and shame that independence was achieved with non-violence and celebrated with violence.

# NOTES